# Toward the Blues

# 33 1/3 Global

**33 1/3 Global**, a series related to but independent from **33 1/3**, takes the format of the original series of short, music-based books and brings the focus to music throughout the world. With initial volumes focusing on Japanese and Brazilian music, the series will also include volumes on the popular music of Australia/Oceania, Europe, Africa, the Middle East, and more.

## 33 1/3 Japan

Series Editor: Noriko Manabe

Spanning a range of artists and genres—from the 1970s rock of Happy End to technopop band Yellow Magic Orchestra, the Shibuya-kei of Cornelius, classic anime series *Cowboy Bebop*, J-Pop/EDM hybrid Perfume, and vocaloid star Hatsune Miku—33 1/3 Japan is a series devoted to in-depth examination of Japanese popular music of the twentieth and twenty-first centuries.

Published Titles:
Supercell's *Supercell* by Keisuke Yamada
*AKB48* by Patrick W. Galbraith and Jason G. Karlin
Yoko Kanno's *Cowboy Bebop Soundtrack* by Rose Bridges
Perfume's *Game* by Patrick St. Michel
Cornelius's *Fantasma* by Martin Roberts
Joe Hisaishi's *My Neighbor Totoro: Soundtrack* by Kunio Hara
Shonen Knife's *Happy Hour* by Brooke McCorkle
Nenes' *Koza Dabasa* by Henry Johnson
Yuming's *The 14th Moon* by Lasse Lehtonen

Forthcoming Titles:
Yellow Magic Orchestra's *Yellow Magic Orchestra* by Toshiyuki Ohwada
Kohaku utagassen: The Red and White Song Contest by Shelley Brunt

## 33 1/3 Brazil

Series Editor: Jason Stanyek

Covering the genres of samba, tropicália, rock, hip hop, forró, bossa nova, heavy metal and funk, among others, 33 1/3 Brazil is a series devoted to in-depth examination of the most important Brazilian albums of the twentieth and twenty-first centuries.

Published Titles:

Caetano Veloso's *A Foreign Sound* by Barbara Browning

Tim Maia's *Tim Maia Racional Vols. 1 &2* by Allen Thayer

João Gilberto and Stan Getz's *Getz/Gilberto* by Brian McCann

Gilberto Gil's *Refazenda* by Marc A. Hertzman

Dona Ivone Lara's *Sorriso Negro* by Mila Burns

Milton Nascimento and Lô Borges's *The Corner Club* by Jonathon Grasse

Racionais MCs' *Sobrevivendo no Inferno* by Derek Pardue

Naná Vasconcelos's *Saudades* by Daniel B. Sharp

Chico Buarque's First *Chico Buarque* by Charles A. Perrone

Forthcoming titles:

Jorge Ben Jor's *África Brasil* by Frederick J. Moehn

## 33 1/3 Europe

Series Editor: Fabian Holt

Spanning a range of artists and genres, 33 1/3 Europe offers engaging accounts of popular and culturally significant albums of Continental Europe and the North Atlantic from the twentieth and twenty-first centuries.

Published Titles:

Darkthrone's *A Blaze in the Northern Sky* by Ross Hagen

Ivo Papazov's *Balkanology* by Carol Silverman

Heiner Müller and Heiner Goebbels's *Wolokolamsker Chaussee* by Philip V. Bohlman

Modeselektor's *Happy Birthday!* by Sean Nye

Mercyful Fate's *Don't Break the Oath* by Henrik Marstal

Bea Playa's *I'll Be Your Plaything* by Anna Szemere and András Rónai

Various Artists' *DJs do Guetto* by Richard Elliott

Czesław Niemen's *Niemen Enigmatic* by Ewa Mazierska and Mariusz Gradowski

Massada's *Astaganaga* by Lutgard Mutsaers

Los Rodriguez's *Sin Documentos* by Fernán del Val and Héctor Fouce
Édith Piaf's *Récital 1961* by David Looseley
Nuovo Canzoniere Italiano's *Bella Ciao* by Jacopo Tomatis
Iannis Xenakis's *Persepolis* by Aram Yardumian
Vopli Vidopliassova's *Tantsi* by Maria Sonevytsky
Amália Rodrigues's *Amália at the Olympia* by Lila Ellen Gray
Forthcoming Titles:
Ardit Gjebrea's *Projekt Jon* by Nicholas Tochka
J.M.K.E.'s *To the Cold Land* by Brigitta Davidjants
Taco Hemingway's *Jarmark* by Kamila Rymajdo

## 33 1/3 Oceania

Series Editors: Jon Stratton (senior editor) and Jon Dale (specializing in books on albums from Aotearoa/New Zealand)

Spanning a range of artists and genres from Australian Indigenous artists to Maori and Pasifika artists, from Aotearoa/New Zealand noise music to Australian rock, and including music from Papua and other Pacific islands, 33 1/3 Oceania offers exciting accounts of albums that illustrate the wide range of music made in the Oceania region.

Published Titles:
John Farnham's *Whispering Jack* by Graeme Turner
The Church's *Starfish* by Chris Gibson
Regurgitator's *Unit* by Lachlan Goold and Lauren Istvandity
Kylie Minogue's *Kylie* by Adrian Renzo and Liz Giuffre
Alastair Riddell's *Space Waltz* by Ian Chapman
Hunters & Collectors's *Human Frailty* by Jon Stratton
The Front Lawn's *Songs from the Front Lawn* by Matthew Bannister
Bic Runga's *Drive* by Henry Johnson
The Dead C's *Clyma est mort* by Darren Jorgensen
Hilltop Hoods' *The Calling* by Dianne Rodger
Ed Kuepper's *Honey Steel's Gold* by John Encarnação
Chain's *Toward the Blues* by Peter Beilharz
Forthcoming Titles:
Screamfeeder's *Kitten Licks* by Ben Green and Ian Rogers
Luke Rowell's *Buy Now* by Michael Brown

# Toward the Blues

Peter Beilharz

Series Editors: Jon Stratton, UniSA Creative, University of South Australia, and Jon Dale, University of Melbourne, Australia

BLOOMSBURY ACADEMIC
NEW YORK · LONDON · OXFORD · NEW DELHI · SYDNEY

BLOOMSBURY ACADEMIC
Bloomsbury Publishing Inc
1385 Broadway, New York, NY 10018, USA
50 Bedford Square, London, WC1B 3DP, UK
29 Earlsfort Terrace, Dublin 2, Ireland

BLOOMSBURY, BLOOMSBURY ACADEMIC and the Diana logo
are trademarks of Bloomsbury Publishing Plc

First published in the United States of America 2023

A catalog record for this book is available from the Library of Congress.

| ISBN: | HB: | 978-1-5013-9013-5 |
|---|---|---|
| | PB: | 978-1-5013-9014-2 |
| | ePDF: | 978-1-5013-9016-6 |
| | eBook: | 978-1-5013-9015-9 |

Series: 33 1/3 Oceania

Typeset by Integra Software Services Pvt. Ltd.
Printed and bound in Great Britian

To find out more about our authors and books visit www.bloomsbury.
com and sign up for our newsletters.

*For Chain: Matt Taylor, Phil Manning, Barry Harvey, Barry Sullivan*

# Contents

*Tracks*  xi
*Preface*  xii

**1    Once Around the Block**  1

**2    Tracks: Text**  15

**3    Before and After: Context**  39

**4    Time and Place: Big Context**  63

**5    Back Pages**  87

*Notes*  99
*Index*  104

# Discography

Chain, *Toward the Blues*

> Australia, September 1971, total time 42.38

> Infinity (Festival) SINL 934295

> Matt Taylor, harp, v; Phil Manning, g, v; Barry Harvey, d; Barry Sullivan, b

> Engineer: John Sayers, TCS Studios, Richmond, Victoria

> Cover: gatefold, card, artwork Ian McCausland; photo Jiva Lawler

# Tracks

1. 32/20 Blues (Robert Johnson)
2. Snatch It Back and Hold It (adapted from the stage version) (Junior Wells)
3. Boogie (Chain)
4. Booze Is Bad News Blues (Chain)
5. Albert Gooses Gonna Turn the Blueses Looses Now (Chain)
6. Black and Blue (album version) (Chain)

# Preface

A word, as my English friends might say, before you read on, or hit the cans. Better yet, do both together: read and listen at the same time.

Where to begin? As musicians may be heard to grumble, starting can be easier than finishing; sometimes you just can't finish a song. It kind of takes over, that riff, the groove. Starting a performance is less straightforward. When an overseas band visits Australia there is often a moment of awkward banter, straight out of the American phrase book: 'Good Evening, Melbawn'; no, it's *Melbun*. A different approach I have seen, for example, with virtuoso guitarist Jeff Beck, said nothing until he said thankyou, waved and walked off; or Tedeschi Trucks, that amazing travelling blues rock revue, who follow a trusty approach in which you play for twenty minutes, warm up and establish presence, then say hello. We know who's boss; an atmosphere is established, there is something of the sacred in the air. The space is fixed; the die is cast. A field of experience is opened.

The approach followed in this book aspires to the Tedeschi Trucks example. Let life follow art! A little intro, a survey, once round the block, then the tracks, or the text, this before the context. Context always matters, time and place, especially if the known unknowns figure prominently. Australia hardly figures on the world rock stage, for example, in a standard reference like Bob Stanley's *Yeah Yeah Yeah*.[1] Australian rock music was the backtrack of our lives, in cities like Melbourne, but it will register little elsewhere. Fifty years ago this was caught up with the fact that most of it was local, and it was delivered and consumed live. This music was not widely distributed, but it was widely produced and enjoyed live, on site. The echoes were local. The lines of feedback into the centres were limited. Our sources were often on vinyl, as well as live or aural, but the new sounds were largely to be heard in clubs. They would disappear into the evening air as we headed off home after, to bed, light-headed, exhilarated. These songs did not carry elsewhere, to the big places where the transatlantic axis ruled.

Here we begin with an entrée, then the music, the tracks, the musical text. There needs to be a back story, but in this little book it comes later, at the back. So we move out through concentric circles, from the music text – the tracks – to the immediate culture, including what came before and after for Chain, and then move onto to the larger Australian setting, Melbourne and the other cities and satellites fifty years ago, the efflorescence of the sixties in the antipodes.

What was the atmosphere of the moment, that which gave it that magic?

What can we expect? Maybe the unexpected. Young musos with jazz skills, often classically trained, using the blues form as the agreed medium, a *techne* itself set at low levels, by today's standards, few gadgets, manual rather than electronic skills and tricks. This is indicative of a magic moment in the studio and in Melbourne's wider music scene, where the crossovers in personnel and style led to a thick culture of jazz, blues and elements of prog rock – the latter, that cerebral period style of arranged and sophisticated avant-garde – all this improvised together in form, held together by riffs, close proximity of audience and musos and an incredible intensity within the walls of those small, sweaty joints, taking refuge from the elements and making creative noise to drive the demons away. There was musical promiscuity, frequent changes in musical partners and busy cultural traffic in ideas, sounds and influences. The city clubs and suburban dives were booming. We seemed to be awash in vinyl from the United States and UK, and much of it consisted of white blues, that next wave after the Stones and Beatles, 1965 rather than 1962. The Beatles and Stones were the groundbreakers; they took us sideways to the Yardbirds, Animals, Pretty Things, then to Paul Butterfield, John Mayall, Canned Heat. Chicago blues was harder to get in Melbourne than country blues: Sonny Terry and Brownie McGhee, Lightnin Hopkins, later Elmore James and Sonny Boy Williamson II, John Lee Hooker. We could listen to *Chicago– The Blues Today*, from 1965, but I do not recall ever seeing the Chess label – Little Walter, or Muddy Waters – in my early teens; we had to wait. On vinyl we then came in a generation on: Buddy Guy and Junior Wells, Otis Rush, Otis Spann. The live scene in Melbourne was more mixed. There were lots of local bands playing R'n'B, emerging prog rock in the clubs, featured in the local indie press and even on TV. Locally, on vinyl we began with singles by bands like the Throb, Missing Links, Wild Cherries, Loved Ones. Chain was a vital actor to emerge from this formative scene, and *Toward the Blues* is the tablet they left behind.

So here is the set list for this book. Chapter 1, Once around the Block, sets the scene, introduces the text, *Toward the Blues*, and the immediate context, Melbourne as a matrix of cultural traffic in the early 70's. Chapter 2, Tracks, directly enters into the music, track by track, with particular interest in sonic details of the tracks themselves. Life is short, and even little books are long. As Melbourne bluesman Chris Wilson used to say to his audience, thanks for coming, I know there are other things you could be doing. If you get this far, dear reader, and listen to the album, my work will be done. But there's more, and the backstory makes a difference. Chain has a history, and Australia too. Chapter 3 develops the context further, but in close compass, travelling either side of *Toward the Blues* historically to see where it came from and what was to follow from Chain at its high point, a few years either side of September 1971. Chapter 4 widens the optic to consider some of the relevant history, political economy and culture of Australia as the broader canvas of this moment. This chapter thickens the historical dimension as well as that of the rock scene and its actors and technologies. So we move from text to context, from micro to macro, from the level of experience to the bigger picture. Chapter 5 is my back pages, as the gig comes to a close, and we acknowledge again the personnel and personalities of Chain, 1-2-3-4, the personal, and gesture to the materials you can read or listen to, if you should choose to follow further curiosity. Read on! as the venue doors close.

# 1   Once Around the Block

The music scene in Melbourne in 1971 cannot easily be condensed. Or, maybe, it can. It was rich, thick and diverse, but also had some common indicators: guitar driven, often musically trained, developed skill sets, technologies that were innovative and loud without drowning the performance. Often this music was like jazz in structure, theme or riff, solos in turn, improv to the max. In the field of *Toward the Blues*, its carriers in the band Chain may be taken to represent the best of the Melbourne scene, even the Australian live music scene around 1971. Its contents speak out for the moment, the scene, its atmosphere. This isn't a universal, so much as a suggestive claim. *Toward the Blues* isn't everything to everybody now, and it certainly wasn't then either. But it simultaneously manages to capture something expressive of the culture of the moment, its creativity and energy, its momentary magic and lasting legacy. So what's the fuss?

What makes an album really special? A concatenation of forces: place, time and circumstance. The right combination of musicians, with the appropriate skill and sympathies; the right technologies, equipment and recording; here, Gretsch drums, Fender guitars, coupled together with the best emerging local amplification, Vase from Brisbane, Strauss from Melbourne. Musos with jazz techniques and capacities. The right material, and interpretation. Management, and engineering that is not too intrusive, and maybe even helpful. The right vibe, or moment – the appropriate stimulants, or relaxants. A reception that includes a crowd or following, a local culture. The right presentation, or aesthetic – expressive visuals: cover art that is expressive of all these factors, and their combination. Above all, perhaps, the right music and musicians, individually brilliant and better than this together; able to hear each other, to listen as well as to play, loud mainly. September 1971 all these came together in Melbourne, when Chain released *Toward the Blues*.

## Who Were Chain? What Was *Toward the Blues*?

Three Brisbane boys: Matt Taylor, Barry Harvey, Barry Sullivan; one from Devonport in Tasmania, Phil Manning, this lot joining together in Melbourne, the live music capital of the period. Melbourne was where the gigs were, where the money was. Hippies? Longhairs. Kids, we might now say, young men in their early twenties – that wonderful age, that magical moment of period innovation led by the youthful Clapton and Hendrix, then Duane Allman. The reinvention, or rediscovery of the electric guitar and all its possibilities. Novelty in conception and execution; imagination, technique and technology combined. New approaches, older music styles folded in together.

Chain was of this moment. It was a period seventies blues band with jazz skills and manoeuvres; kind of a prog band, on the cusp of Oz pub rock but not of it. Short-lived, in this classic line-up – around eleven months, within 1971, though there have been numerous iterations of Chain across fifty years, and the Taylor–Manning format is still alive and kicking, playing together when they can. They were named Chain by their one time vocalist, the iconic Wendy Saddington, with possible reference to Aretha Franklin: 'Chain of Fools'. As a young fan and follower of Chain, I had always imagined it was rather a reference to do with the idea of solidarity – all the links fit, no band without the links that fit so snug they seemed to know each other's minds, to know as if by inspiration or intuition what the others would do, to play into each other and make up this sonic chain.

*Toward the Blues* is a classic, and not only because it is recognized as such. It is a time capsule; a window into a moment of innovation and the extension of the electric blues tradition; and it is also an accident, recorded in a difficult week of sessions when the vibe was elusive, came late and in a cloud of marijuana smoke. Whisky helped. Volume. Sympathy. Edge.

There was a hit single that helped carry the album, if it needed carriage. This was 'Black and Blue', which was also included on the album at management insistence, in a period when other leading Australian prog bands like Spectrum refused in principle to pollute the purity of the concept album with the commercial aroma of the single. 'Black and Blue' is a convict work song, the closest Chain got to an anthem, the singalong chorus which later became a staple of pub rock nights. It fit the moment of cultural nationalism which formally was crowned by the election of the reforming Whitlam Labor Government in December 1972. These were watershed days for Australian rock. They were heady days, in a place that was often styled hitherto as a backwater, victim of the tyranny of distance, always a bit too far away from the centres really to matter much. 'Black and Blue' is powerfully local or regional in inflexion. This did not prevent Manfred Mann covering and adapting the song in 1973. The cover was flattering, but the original is better. A sharper cut was offered twenty years later by veteran Oz rocker Jimmy Barnes on the album *Earth Music*, 1994. It is a stadium screamer, characteristically Jimmy, suggestive of the unlocked power of the song and its creators. The original is more austere, and reminds you how important Matt's harp is to the Chain effect.

'Black and Blue' was out of character for the Australian Top 40 in 1971, with two significant exceptions. Blues rock wasn't exactly the stuff of hits. That year's hit list was relatively dull, mainstream international acts like Tony Orlando and the Partridge Family. The local exceptions to hit the charts were Daddy Cool, 'Eagle Rock' and 'I'll Be Gone'. Impresario Michael Gudinski was yet to break Skyhooks; at first the leading entrepreneur was also a kid, literally a schoolboy organizing gigs around the city of Melbourne. Gudinski rode to the top with bands like Skyhooks, later Kylie Minogue. Unlike these later acts and their sense of spectacle, Chain was all about the music. And this was transformative for Gudinski, who later wrote that 'Matt Taylor and Chain were a major influence in my life. I was 17 going on 18 when I became their manager … It was Chain's influence that had a big impact on me when I started working with Muddy Waters', and all the rest of the global crew.[1]

Chain was no glam rock band, nor did they wear lounge suits like the visitors from Chicago. They were old school hippy, T-shirts and jeans as a matter of principle, a sign of refusal of the conformist sounds that came with the cheesy cabaret matching velvet suits and fancy dental work that swamped the airwaves meantime. And the message was in the album, not the singalong single.

But if Chain were a measure of their moment, they were also not alone. Their music came out of a situation and a scene, a matrix of players and actors like Gudinski who also made it happen. *Toward the Blues* had its local parallels, in 1971. Local bands of the year include Daddy Cool, Spectrum, Masters Apprentices in their third album, Russell Morris, the Aztecs, and Blackfeather. A motley crew – Daddy Cool combining punch, doo wop and residues of Zappa on *Daddy Who?*; Spectrum the perfect cool concert band, Masters at a peak with tougher songs and guitar ace Doug Ford sharp but restrained. *Bloodstone*, a showcase of Melbourne studio talents including Chain and singer songwriter Brian Cadd and the formative Bootleg project behind Russell Morris, the Aztecs live pushing the amps to 13, more Blue Cheer than blues cheers, Blackfeather *At the Mountains of Madness*, massive hair, loud wooden school recorders over louder guitar (recorders were big, then to be superseded by flutes). *Toward the Blues* was something else, edge, finesse, improv and self-control all mixed up in one.

What was *Toward the Blues*? This was the text: six tracks, forty-three minutes, delivered live in the studio, like a gig, or a jam of a particular kind – disciplined, actually. Live with dubs, as legendary guitar hero Lobby Loyde would later put it. As Lobby liked to say, the heart and soul of the musical experience is live – the band clicks, the audience clicks, they all click together, and the joint is jumping. There were several rings of concentric context around this. There was a prehistory, to the band and their recording, and a posthistory, what followed on from this moment and its line-up. There was an Australian history, and a global history around it. And for the purposes of this telling, there was a smaller, personal history for me. I knew Chain, as much as a boy follower might; my band played support for them. We talked back then, and I interviewed Phil Manning extensively now, for this project, fifty years later, looking back to remember and to make sense of it all, to remember when we were young.

Chain also, then, had a history, or a prehistory. It took in another colonial city, alongside Brisbane: Perth, and the band Beat'n Tracks, led by Warren Morgan and including before Phil, Dave Hole, later to become the wild slider. Warren travelled east. Barry Sullivan and Barry Harvey headed south, from a band called Thursday's Children to Melbourne. Manning had travelled north, from Tasmania, then west to Perth and back to Melbourne. Vital to this story, Sullivan switched from guitar to bass, and spent months learning this craft rehearsing alone with Harvey, on drums. These were serious and formative links and bonds. They became two of a kind.

So Chain resulted from cultural traffic, the movement between places and cities interspersed by other influences, many of them coming on vinyl after the British Rock invasion; maybe it was a second invasion, after 1788.

Chain also had a previous recording history. There were some hits and misses at pop singles, some echoes of Traffic and the Band, and some blues or R n B in the form of the Brisbane band Bay City Union, which first brought together Manning and Taylor in Melbourne in 1967, on Port Phillip Bay. The bigger bang, something of a cult item to carry under your arm to local record parties then was the album *Live Chain*, 1970. Some of this stuff was pretty outrageous, by the standard of the three-minute seven-inch records that ruled the Top 40. Five long experimental tracks. It was not just jam; most of the arrangements were by Morgan, an extensively trained jazz player, with the multiple sequences and clever time changes and elaborate solos which came to characterize prog rock. Howzat!

*Live Chain* was a five piece – two guitars, add Glyn Mason; Manning, Morgan and Barry Harvey with Barry Sullivan. Barnyard nicknames caught on – the Barries were Big and

Little Goose, apparently as the sharpie gang called their like long-haired gooses; Morgan was the Pig. Only Phil and Matt escaped nicknames in the long run. The album was a mix of blues, jazz and sequenced ballads with stronger vocal lines. It was amazing, Phil on Gibson Stereo sailing over the Pig's little Hohner Clavinet. This was the first version of Chain I saw, at the Traffik disco in Flinders Lane near Spencer Street fifty years ago, at fifteen or so, in the company of my friend Vivian Lees, himself later to become a leading rock entrepreneur.

Skip forward. By the moment of *Toward the Blues*, a year later, and the classic fourpiece line-up, we have Taylor on harp and vocal, Manning carrying rhythm and lead lines and also singing, the Geese in the most amazing lockstep rhythm section ever seen in the history of Australian rock. The edge was closer to boogie, but the compositions were originals or improvs, blows or variations on standards inspired by Robert Johnson's '32/20' or Junior Wells's 'Snatch it Back'. These latter, however, were more like adaptations than derivations. Improv was central, and it kept the mood of the performance closer to jazz than to the blues which provided riffs and grooves for the musicians to work around and build upon.

The album opened with '32/20 Blues', a Johnson classic which had remained largely neglected in the white blues wave which selected other Johnson songs but relied perhaps especially heavily on the electric slide licks of his follower, Elmore James. Quick time, double track guitar solo in octaves. 'Snatch it Back,' a little slower, with the cheek of Junior Wells and then some. 'Boogie' was to follow. It became a staple of white blues, popularized by LA bands like Canned Heat in the wake of John Lee Hooker, here delivered by Chain in a manner that was more tasteful and bounded than the period live excess of Canned Heat. 'Booze Is Bad News Blues' is the most scintillating of the tracks on *Toward the Blues*, slow blues, a lament soaring especially in Manning's central guitar solo, again double tracked, with slide, tremolo and wah, but especially that bend which would take you close to breaking. 'Albert Gooses' is Barry Harvey's second recorded drum solo, built into licks and riffs that sustain its own sense of cool, which frame it and place it within the band's general commitment to improv. The solo is not a workout; it is conceptual and nuanced. It works, like Joe Morello on 'Take Five'. The album closes with 'Black and Blue'. Not the band's idea for inclusion here, this single had been separately recorded earlier in Sydney. The reluctant compromise was to cut the song afresh, so that it would at least be continuous with the flow of the album, in what had gone before, so the album would be of a piece, not a dumpster.

How did all this come together? As I shall explain below, the most essential ingredient in the magic was the combination of musical talents, sympathies and material. The core of Chain was the trio, guitar/bass/drums, and within this the rhythm section of the Geese. Lockstep! Matt Taylor floated over this with harp and vocal and jokes and banter, and a lyrical presence that capitalized on a deep range, as though his voice was also an instrument. Their material was new and exciting; but the core players could all read music, and all played jazz; old school. They were to become the most respected session players in Australian rock history. Barry Harvey (Little Goose) on drums, could not only read but also write charts, going on to attend the Berklee School of Music in Boston and publish a primer on polyrhythms called *The Text of Music Phrase* (1995).[2] Big Goose (Barry Sullivan) became the bass player most often compared in Australia to James Jamerson, that amazing Motown lead where the roles of bass and guitar were reversed. Phil became the most respected Australian blues and roots guitar player ever. Note perfect, guitar royalty, as my guitarist friends would say.

Chain was one of the first bands to attract the enthusiasm of the youthful entrepreneur Michael Gudinski, though *Toward* was already underway when he signed the band, before he started Mushroom records initially to promote Chain and alternative rock. He then began, among other things, to deliver a steady flow of oversea blues acts to Australia, including Muddy Waters, BB King, Hound Dog Taylor, Freddie King, Willie Dixon and many more. Chain was often the support, and came to collaborate with members of Muddy's band. All this was to follow, as was Gudinski's album anthologization of *The History of Chain* (1974). For if Gudinski came to make his big money with big names, he began and persisted with the kind of underground music that first turned on his lights, and mine. With Chain, his recipe seemed to be simple: let them play what they liked, trust their own creative approaches, and score them so many weekly gigs at self-organized venues that they would be finessed in no time. It worked: drop the coin right in the slot. Perfect timing, again; ten years later Gudinski would be working popular entertainment rather than this avant-garde.

As it had a prehistory, *Toward the Blues* also had a history after. Across the decades the album slowly went Gold, the award finally arriving in 1998. It was followed by two more albums from the continuous line-up, or three, if you count Matt Taylor's *Straight as a Die*, 1973. *Toward* was followed by *Chain Live Again*, which directly duplicated the 1970 line-up. Some of the improv moments here were close to the earlier peaks, but the songs were half hearted in contrast to those on *Toward*, as in 'Pig's Blues'. There were contractual obligations to fulfil.

More innovative musically was *Two of a Kind*, 1973, though this was also a sort of accidental arrival, combining one side of the expanded Chain line-up, adding Ian Clyne on keys and Mal Capewell on reeds, together with slip-slidin guitar guest Greg 'Sleepy' Lawrie. This line-up played one side as an 18' 32" track, a psychedelic fusion instrumental titled 'How to Set Fire to an Elephant', including Harvey's third recorded drum solo. The other side featured two touring members of Muddy Waters' band, James Madison and George Buford, playing the title song and other standards such as 'Blues with a Feeling'. The different players mesh, all this welded together by the ease of the rhythm section, which glides. *Straight as a Die* is a kind of proxy, final Chain album, though others were to follow from other reformations over the years. Recorded live outdoors at Taylor's Frankston farm on the outskirts of Melbourne, it featured the *Toward the Blues* line-up and Sleepy Lawrie on guitar. The music was unmistakably Taylor's, lyrics touting vegetarianism, Krishna consciousness and the art of living simply. Its attendant single became the final proxy Chain anthem, 'I Remember When I Was Young'.

As there is text, there is also social and historical context. We can glimpse the immediate context here, and return to the longer and larger context in Chapter 4.

*Toward the Blues* also had its immediate history in the emerging Australia of the 70's. Graham Freudenberg, Prime Minister Whitlam's speechwriter from 1972, used to joke that the 60's arrived in Australia in the 70's. He was at least half right. Chain was part of a moment in Australian history which we now regard as inextricably caught up with radical politics, the opposition to the Vietnam War, hippie culture, very long hair and its attendant fashion codes, peace, love and marijuana. The key Chain song of the period did not make it onto the album, or any other. It was called 'My Arse Is Black with Bourke Street', what Taylor would call a boompa boompa, 12 bar as in 'Dust My Blues', or a variation thereupon. It was an antiwar song celebrating the Vietnam Moratorium movement, which had closed down Bourke Street, Melbourne's central artery, with a massive sit-in demonstration of 100,000 souls in 1970. Chain was a vital part of the music scene that went with this counterculture. Blue jeans turned black with the bitumen. We went in our school uniforms to the demo, and to the concert that followed in Treasury Gardens. Matt Taylor followed this alternative, or counterculture impulse through most fully, forsaking performance for communal living first in Beechworth in Victoria and later in Balingup in the south of Western Australia. We went back to school, to complete year 11, awaiting possible call-up, compulsory conscription, to follow when we hit 18. We lived in hope, and in fear.

The final concentric circle here is that of global context. Australian culture was often thought to be too far away from where the action was. An alternative view is that distance, or being on the periphery can also be an advantage when it comes to innovation. What was happening that was new in the global music scene in 1971? In a word, prog; but there is always more. John Hepworth provides a dossier in *1971–Never a Dull Moment*. Hepworth's is an interesting approach, not least as he flags Carole King's *Tapestry* as a key work, both in style and content and in audience – girls.[3] Chain was clearly a boys' band. Its demographic was largely male, if often with girlfriends. For boys in the audience, there was some kind of male spectatorship crossing into musical connoisseurship. A little swaying, maybe; no dancing. Audiences would stand, in club settings, or sit in hippie scenes, sometimes bringing blankets and cushions and even small children. This was the Love Generation.

The standout echo in Hepworth's scan is something different. 1971 was the year the Allman Brothers Band did the Fillmore East, in what may be one of the greatest live albums ever. The differences are also striking. The Allmans is a power project: two very loud guitars, two drummers – one jazz, one rock, super volume and supercharged Hammond B3. The music was brilliant, the playing superb, also jazz and blues, but it was something of an assault. Chain, in contrast, was a combo, a jazz unit playing blues forms, three plus one rather than two plus two plus. Club, rather than stadia. Two years earlier, a parallel might be seen in the debut Columbia album of Johnny Winter. Phil Manning was also a borderline albino, but he was not a guitar hero, in this manner or that of Allman or Alvin Lee or Santana. He was a brilliant soloist, but first of all a band member. He played direct, like Winter, without the battery of effects that was soon to become obligatory. Step up, cut loose, note perfect; step back; that was Chain. Every link mattered. The band was brilliant, and they were ours. We could listen, and watch them sweat, talk after, learn by example.

For finally, there was a small personal story here. Chain was the source of my musical initiation, the period of *Live Chain* and then *Toward the Blues*. By the time of the latter, my band, Serenity, was supporting Chain in high school halls in the outer eastern suburbs of Melbourne. We would talk, especially with Phil, who had the decency to treat us as equals even though we were novices. Fifty years later I would take the train to his home in West Footscray to talk through all this, not least *Toward the Blues* track by track. How did you get that sound? and so on. And he would pick up his Strat and show me.

But to begin, what was it that happened when we stumbled into Melbourne clubs like Traffik or the Thumpin Tum, evading those burly bouncers, alcohol concealed about our persons, wearing those giveaway army disposal store greatcoats in summer? What was it that happened when we sat cross-legged at home in front of my brother's bass amp, and dropped that chipped sapphire needle on the first track of the album? What was it about this kind of live music, or its direct to disc rendition? What was *Toward the Blues*?

# **2** Tracks: Text

Drop the coin right in the slot/You gonna hear something that's really hot/Drop that needle on the vinyl/Punch that handset, Head for spotify/Turn it up, in any case. Be ready to move, or at least tap that foot, bop a little. Chain swings. You can dance if you want, as Melbourne blues harp king Chris Wilson used to beckon his crowd two decades later. Even with jump blues, they tended not to jump, but rather to stand and look cool, just like it was still 1971. We stood, tapped feet, listened, clapped, were buzzed away, transported, our flares moving to the sonic pressure coming out of those big speaker boxes. You could get up close, feel and smell it, patchouli, tobacco and weed.

What happens when you listen at home, or in company, let that needle drop? It's not standard rock and roll, Jimmy Reed, Chuck Berry, in Oz rendition AC/DC. *Toward the Blues* is not a pop record. Unlike the common earlier format of twelve songs, by three minutes apiece, it has six tracks from the original TCS sessions in Richmond, an inner suburb of Melbourne, recorded by John Sayers on eight-track, released in September 1971. This album was conceived as a piece, in a sense of musical integrity, as the first five tracks. The hit single 'Black and Blue' was added into the final cut under pressure from management. In order to maintain their intended integrity or purpose the band recorded 'Black and Blue' afresh, as part of the TCS recording sessions. The hit single was recorded earlier, in Sydney, at the Festival studios in Pyrmont. The releasing label, symptomatically called Infinity, was Festival's alternative rock line. This was just before the boom achieved by Australia's leading indy label, Mushroom, steered by Michael Gudinski.

Fans and players alike know that the moment of opening matters, live or on the deck. The first track, that opening song of the night, like Tedeschi Trucks sets the mood for all that follows. Remember, the template or intended mood for the album is live. So here Chain began with '32/20 Blues'. This is now widely known to us as a Robert Johnson song, though there are precedents, such as Skip James's earlier piano version, '22/20'.

Robert Johnson became the mythical origin of the American blues story as it was relayed into the mainstream by white players three decades later. Twenty-nine tracks recorded in Dallas and San Antonio hotels 1936–7; these songs featured acoustic slide with a sometimes ghostly voice floating over it, as in 'Sweet Home Chicago'. For many less receptive it was the music of the devil. The Robert Johnson songbook became widely available, for connoisseurs of the blues, with the release of the John Hammond Snr Columbia collection *King of the Delta Blues Singers* in 1961. Many of these songs found their way into the white canon, most famously the radically reworked 'Crossroads' for Cream in 1968, *Wheels of Fire – Live at the Fillmore*. '32/20' remained low profile until Clapton and Peter Green developed their own Robert Johnson songbooks into the twenty-first century. Chain were among the first to take on '32/20' decades earlier. John Hammond Jr covered the song, acoustic, in 1965. The Flamin Groovies covered it fairly closely as a shuffle in 1971, Government Mule rather later. Dylan then covered the song in a clean acoustic version collected on his bootleg series, *Tell Tale Signs* twenty years after Chain. Chain turned it into something else. As with Cream and other interpretations, 'I'm So Glad', 'Four Until Late' or 'Spoonful', the electrically charged version is barely recognizable against the original. All that travels, in the sonics, is the riff, if that. These renditions are worlds apart, in both time and place, and yet there is some kind of continuity in the adaptation. And for a generation of white kids, there was the new imperative to go back, to go to the roots. So we listened to Chain, and Cream, and sought out Robert Johnson. Rock music was also a matter of discovery and retrieval.

Chain's version of '32/20' is in the key of C and runs at 4/4 time. It begins with guitar and drums, Matt's harp and vocal to follow, Phil joining in on vocals in unison, then the bass line powers in at the fourth verse. Harp and guitar are as tightly paired as are bass and drums. Matt and Phil jump together. Phil's guitar solo is double tracked, with a third line dropped in later. The song is carried by bass and drums. Drums accelerate in locomotive manner, snare single and double stroke, bass drum doubling tripling as it goes, bass guitar in sync with bass drum. Drum fill and hand claps are added, bass trippin' like Motown.

It is not quite a murder ballad, but it is a gun song, with murderous intent, symbolized by a Winchester piece, the 32/20 itself.[1] Its lyric concerns revenge killing for betrayal, real or imagined; the woman victim is also armed, with a .38 special, but that's 'much too light.' The 32/20 is lethal, like a crosscut saw, cuts your victim half in two. Listening to this in Melbourne fifty years ago I guess we might have connected it to 'Hey Joe', the lyrics of which also seemed bizarre to us; who would actually shoot someone? for Australia has never had a gun culture like that so deeply ingrained in the history and culture of the United States. The image echoes weakly in Australia, where there are nevertheless serious issues with domestic violence. It has been suggested that the lyric is a proxy, that the object of a possible killing would rather be the white man, the big boss man, who also shows up elsewhere, as in Jimmy Reed. A good song for context here, in this endless field of interpretation, would be Johnson's 'Hellhound on my Trail'; no metaphors apply. Pursued by police dogs and lynch gangs, a gun might look like a friend. There are Australian echoes, including the massacres of Aboriginal peoples, the hunting parties and murders. As for '32/20', its lyrics are best left behind. After 1969 we were with John and Yoko, singing Give Peace a Chance. Call us liberals, radicals, hippies, whatever: didn't want no guns.

The second track is inspired by the 1965 Junior Wells song 'Snatch It Back and Hold It'. It's an interesting track to play back, originally off Junior's prizewinning *Hoodoo Man Blues* in 1965. The song had been around, though only in cult circles. Local band Adderley Smith had recorded an earlier version on a demo in 1967. Junior's line-up anticipates Chain's directly – Buddy Guy on the thinner twang of the Stratocaster at less than full volume, and lockstep session bass and drums, Jack Myers and Bill Warren. Chain's song bounces off Junior's lyrics, but features a differently accentuated riff. Chain deliver in the key of G, again 4/4. As Matt would make clear in the banter at gigs, this sexual enthusiasm in the lyrics was understood to be mutual and consensual. This may have been the entendre of Junior's original, but that version was also a kind of blues take on James Brown, 'Papa's Got a Brand New Bag', usually taken to refer to a dance step, though in this field dance was never far away from sex: rock and roll. The two songs are strikingly different, as is Chain's '32/20' from Robert Johnson. The track opens with a train song line, a common electric blues line in the period – snare roll speeding up and slowing down, harp and guitar hooting and sliding over three bass notes and accelerating and then relaxing drum patterns. Bass guitar is thick, doubletracked, a trick also employed by the Beatles on 'While My Guitar', and by Lou Reed on 'Walk on the Wild Side'. Phil's guitar weaves deftly; it follows the Buddy Guy–chitlin circuit chicken pickin', one of those novelty guitar effects which can be found earlier on disc for example on 'Chicken Hearted Woman' by Clarence Samuels in 1956. But it also adds voice, and bend, and pitch. Here Phil is playing not the red Stratocaster which appears on the cover photo of the album, but a Telecaster modified by Phil with a Fender Jaguar tremolo arm fitted with the aid of a hammer and chisel, P90 pickups, this before he enlisted the services of Melbourne guitar whiz Merv Cargill for added finesse. Phil also later reversed the angle of the bridge pickup on the Strat L Series, so the contact was closer to the bass strings, as in Hendrix; he was evidently keen on experiment. There is some suggestion of country picking in the guitar in the tone here, but also a firmer blues guitar line that echoes Clapton's rendition of 'Crossroads'.

Track Three is simply called 'Boogie'. It is a fast 12/8, in the key of G. Boogie had become a standard item in the repertoire of white blues bands into the 70's, mediated by John Lee Hooker and then most popularly by LA band Canned Heat, for whom the item eventually became a staple, played long and hard, more than thirty minutes long with solos for each and all in turn. Chain is sometimes thought of as a boogie band, but this title would better go to local blues band Carson, whose boogies were thickened out by piano or Hammond B3 and sometimes sax. The Chain boogie, like the band, was lean. Phil leads on the Tele, adding a Vox Cry Baby or wah wah pedal. It opens with bass and guitar exchanging lines, a build-up, drums slide in, still slow, then thickening till the 12/8 takes off. The slide part is overdubbed, and guitar echo is added in via the mixing board. Phil's memory is that some of the overlay was on the Tele, but the heavier contours are delivered on the Strat. Bass and drums are lockstep, and become thicker as the song progresses. It's a standard Chain blow – a riff that leads to a jam, with words added over the top, the standard images of sexual excess, vagrancy, police cars, drug abuse and desolation, 'lying in a gutter all shot up with speed' etc. Matt had had his share of trouble with the police in Brisbane – it wasn't hard to achieve. The Deep North was infamous for conservative government and corrupt police. His girly long hair had been forcibly cut off in the station house, and like other young Australian men of the time he knew well to keep clear of the cops. But this was not the world of 'Hellhound on My Trail'. It involved harassment, not lynching. Brisbane was not Mississippi, even if it felt like 'Pig City', or a police state to its younger inhabitants into the 70's.[2] It was the kind of place the Saints would feel stranded in.

Track four is Phil's song, 'Booze Is Bad News Blues'. It opens in a way reminiscent of the mood of Derek and the Dominoes version of 'Key to the Highway'. But where producer Tom Dowd was by repute caught napping, while the band had already begun, and the Dominos ease in, the voice of the engineer for Chain, John Sayers, can barely be heard to say 'roll the tape'. The band was jamming, after all. Little Goose remembers that he was so out of it that he thought this was a gig for friends, not a recording session but a private party that just happened to be in a recording studio. He remembered the track as a warm-up; reminds us, in retrospect, of Tedeschi Trucks, warming up, setting the mood for what is to follow. Phil remembers the week of available time being complicated to begin, wasted days, whisky and weed, and then … click. It all fell into place, three or four magical hours, the octaves added later on. Little Goose remembers playback, the day after. He thought the track was

great but did not recognize who it was playing. 'That's great –
is that us?' This is another 12/8, but slow, painfully slow for
Phil as we listen back to it together fifty years later; these days
he doubles the tempo when revisiting the song live around
the traps. You can find a more recent version on *Chain – The
First Thirty Years*, a live compilation assembled by Phil. It bops.
For the original, key of E, standard blues pitch. Phil sings the
opening verses, plays slide. It's a lazy blues, Phil and Matt again
loping along together with the ease of an old couple. Guitar
and vocals is nestled along by Matt's harp, which swirls and
supports, indicating the incredible sympathy between Matt
and Phil. Unlike 'Key to the Highway', it is original, following
a general slow blues pattern rather than a pre-established
template. The lyrics are plaintive, confessional, almost even
redemptive:

> I started drinking in the bar/Sure gets you where you know/
> The more you drink, faster your senses go/or, Faster your
> money goes …

– the latter varied to living goes, or liver goes

'We were all very stoned by this stage!' says Phil. Matt takes
three verses in his deeper intonation and broad Australian
twang, and harp solo.

Matt takes over, stronger voice, Australian drawl, bending
the vocal range:

> All that whisky, gin and wine/Have given me a good time/
> But as I look back I swear it was a nasty crime/You know my
> baby left me?/She did not even say one word …

Matt varies good good for bad, bad, and nasty for good, live.
Improv works for lyrics as well as sonics. Matt was a raver. The

end of the storyline is abstinence, 'no more bad news blues' for the time being at least. Until tomorrow.

Bass and drums here are lockstep as usual, with little embellishment; one note on the Jazz Bass just under the fret, for emphasis, and glissando across two of the cymbals, ride and splash, understated as ever. The crescendo is in Phil's guitar solo. The Fenders sing. Phil uses Lobby's turbocharged 240-watt Strauss Warrior, six KT 88 valves and eight or a dozen twelve-inch speakers. Four verses of guitar solo, the first bursts over the verse line, the second beautifully lyrical, the third the stuff of goosebumps, one more on slide to follow, or exit. The third uses slide and wah, but when I asked Phil how he got that blistering sound – tremolo, too? he leaned over, picked up his Strat, unplugged and showed me. It's all in the bend! says he. And in the strings, Black Diamond or Gibson, following the young Clapton trick of using a banjo string on E. Phil explains that by virtue of its key, E, he was able to play the solo originally with open B and open E top strings ringing, bringing on a droning effect accentuated with gentle vibrato on the tremolo arm, the melody line then added to later in octave. This is a moment of rare and chilling beauty in period Oceanic rock, paralleled perhaps only by Lindsay Wells on Healing Force's 'Golden Miles' or Billy Green on Doug Parkinson's 'Dear Prudence', both of which are more pacific. And then some, for the solo sits stark in its context. Bass and drums tag and mark the solo, but guitar cuts through like a knife, like the knife blade that earlier players used as a slide.

Slide was maybe a late starter in the blues rock scene in Australia. Who then played slide? The use of slide or bottleneck did not have a long local recorded history. In rock, there was the lacerating slide of Norm Roué and Phil Key in Band of Light (– try 'Destiny Song'), later Kevin Borich and Pete Wells and a younger generation of blues purists like Jeff Lang and Geoff Achison who developed slide into a local art form.

Phil taught himself slide. It took a while, as there was nobody to learn from, no elder to instruct him about retuning the guitar to open key. Phil's mate Sleepy Lawrie has a similar recall. Go to hardware store, buy a length of curtain rod, cut it with a hacksaw, make it up as you go along. As Sleepy remembers, the only slide guitars around were pedal steel, lovely instruments but another ballgame altogether, Hawaiian or bluegrass, Speedy West or maybe C 'n' W. Sleepy was also listening to Library of Congress blues files, the Texans, Lowell Fulson, T Bone Walker. Sleepy made slide his thing.[3] Slide was a trick in Phil's box, rather than a way of life for him as a picker. But it's hard to disagree when he shows you, and we laugh – it's in the bend! The power of the tone is manual, *manus*, the hand. Phil Manus.

When I asked Phil about slide, he volunteered Jeff Beck and Muddy Waters as obvious later influences. Generations apart – Muddy tough and sharp, Jeff eloquent and more given to nuance. Earlier, Phil was inspired by Robert Johnson, Skip James, and Blind Willie McTell, mostly open tuning as he had worked it out. By the time Duane Allman, Ry Cooder and Bonnie Raitt had transformed the North American reception of slide, Phil and Sleepy were already self-taught. So, for that matter, was Duane, as the story goes, listening not to the original of Blind Willie McTell but to Jesse Ed Davis on Taj Mahal's 1968 rendition of 'Statesboro Blues', adapting that standard yellow American pill bottle as the ratchet. (Who taught Derek Trucks?)

Sliding along, the fifth track is likely the most original. 'Albert Goose Is Gonna Let the Blueses Looses Now', Matt announces in that Aussie drawl after an introductory tag. It's a beautiful, tasteful drum solo with music dropped in around it and over it. The track opens with drums, 12/8. Key of G. The mood is jazzy – playing time on ride cymbal, punctuation improvised on snare, always played by Little Goose in jazz grip, picking out the accents, bass drum played alternating against the snare, shaft of the right stick across the ride cymbal on the third stroke, some rimshot. Then guitar and bass re-enter, and finally harp. Bass and drums perform some wonderful intuitive layering and tricks together. Big Goose uses the Jazz Bass he learned on and stuck with until Maton Guitars made him a BG bass, and a 200-w Vase, 6 × 12 inch speakers, 2 × 15. Little Goose by now has had his own PA built by Vase, four close mikes, 4 × 12 in two columns. Loud, but crisp, and focused, the kind of clarity and control you could never get from the house PA or a single mike across the bass drum on top, as was common then.

Now Little Goose cuts loose. Phil tells me it is his least favourite track in terms of his own performance; he claims he himself never could play jazz! I beg to differ, reminding him of the lovely Wes Montgomery riffs, octaves, on the first Chain album, on the track 'Black and White', the cooler forerunner to 'Black and Blue'. Phil observes that this kind of line can be hard to carry; the earlier five piece line-up was smoother for him, with Warren Morgan vamping on piano, and Phil free of the dual task of carrying both lead and rhythm instruments as well as singing. He adds that the fourpiece was great, like the five piece, because the other players were better than him, more accomplished, not least at jazz. Phil Manning is uncharacteristically modest for a rock muso; again, I choose to disagree, as we listen and talk, but he has a point, that the others provide lift, and make so much possible, in a magical moment like this. The trick was in the combination, and the capacity.

Matt observes:

> We played blues, but we played like a jazz band, with a feel.
> If you look at the songs on *Toward The Blues*, the 'Boogie'
> was never practised. 'Booze is Bad News Blues' was also
> never practised. We'd just get up on stage and play …
> We'd never seen a black blues band. Come to think of it …
> we'd never seen a white blues band from overseas … In their
> approach, the guys in Chain played more like a jazz band, it
> was mostly improvised with self imposed discipline.[4]

They were extraordinary musos. As Brittany Jenke observes,
writing about the album for the *Rolling Stone Australian 200
Greatest Australian Albums of All Time* fifty years on, … 'it was
more than just a good album, it stood tall as a masterpiece
of Aussie blues-rock, capturing the era of hazy, boozy pub
gigs in country towns, and a visceral recollection of a time
when stellar musicianship reigned supreme'.[5] The album
scraped in at #197, not bad considering the explosion of rock
music that erupted over the fifty years that followed. But the
punchline stands: this was stellar musicianship.[6] Chain really
were remarkably able musicians, even in 1971, in their youth.
This was already recognized earlier, in O'Donnell, Creswell,
Mathieson *Best 100 Australian Albums*, where *Toward the Blues*
comes in at 67. 'Chain was the ultimate Australian blues/rock
band … far and away the best Australian blues album, ever' …
as good as Cream? they wondered.[7] 'NO!' says Phil fifty years
on; though he had already then moved on from the Clapton
fave, the Gibson Stereo, because it made everything sound too
Creamy. Fenders were more versatile.

Guitars ruled in this budding scene. There were lots of bands
in a city like Melbourne, beat bands, and they were ordinary,
as elsewhere. Certainly anybody with a few quid could buy a

cheap guitar into the 60's, and work on those three chords, or at least some rudimentary version of a tune like 'Peter Gunn'. You would frequently meet amateurs who had formed bands even though they couldn't yet play themselves; maybe their indulgent parents had spent big money on gear they didn't deserve. There were fewer drummers around, partly because of the cost of the kit and its non-portability, unless you also could borrow the family wagon. There was no shortage of plain drummers among those around, metronomic at best. All the same, drummers were more in the spotlight than before. Drum solos became routine in these times, almost obligatory, like boogies. They were often poorly executed, closer to the gym or workout than musical experiment. Little Goose, as we have seen, was an exceptional drummer and musician. He works around the kit, but understates, and works in patterns on the cymbals. This is serious business, no messing round. As he wrote later in his own drum text:

> The hi-hat is the *most diverse* of the cymbals because of the use of the foot as a note. It is definitely an *incredible invention* and there are no limits to the techniques of playing that can be created with it.[8]

His hands and feet were dancing, a visual as well as sonic feat. He was known, in this time, to deliver an entire live solo on cymbals; high-risk behaviour, if the crowd was unruly or impatient. He spreads out, and finally, on the *Toward the Blues* solo, he counts out, 1 2 3 1 2 3 and the band closes with another tag.

Tags were a Chain hallmark in live performance. The theme from the Mickey Mouse Club Mouseketeers – Annette Funicello and Frankie Avalon – 'Quando Quando', Happy Birthday, the barnyard chicken strut, the harp led police siren – cops, beware!

Run away! Typically this was a chitlin circuit signal to the crowd that the band was about to start or finish, maybe take a break. Or else to be funny, and Matt was to become the master of banter, with endless jokes about the tedious and endlessly repeated recipe of Elmore James, the boompa boompa, which the band also revelled in. But not on *Toward the Blues*. The album was conceived as a live performance with dubs. It was not part of the plan to close with a second, live version of 'Black and Blue'. There are no jokes on *Toward the Blues*, even though Matt used to vary the lyrics for example of 'Black and Blue', as in 'I miss ma whiskey and I miss ma fish' … *Toward the Blues* was serious, at least on the record.

'Black and Blue' was to become an anthem, even when the chorus, 'we're groaning', was misheard as 'Where's Rosie?' Matt tells of receiving requests for the latter from keen enthusiasts who had completely missed the convict lament, taking it rather for a love song for somebody called Rosie. Matt had long had a notion to write a work song, not quite a holler but a convict work song. In the years around and after the publication of Robert Hughes's *The Fatal Shore* in 1987 it became more common to observe that Australia was a dual prison, based on the punishment of Indigenous peoples and incarcerated colonial convicts alike. It is possible, however, that Vietnam was such a big thing, threatening white boys with conscription as well as the lives of the Vietnamese people at home, that it was allowed to overshadow Indigenous rights until later. 1971 was in any case a significant moment in the emergence of the new cultural nationalism, crowned by the election of the Whitlam Government in December 1972. The iconic image here now is less 'It's Time', Whitlam's 1972 slogan, than the photo of Whitlam with Gurindji leader Vincent Lingiari returning a handful of the soil of the land to the original inhabitants in 1975.

This was a period of transition in which cultural experimentation, for example in the new wave of film in *Walkabout*, *Wake in Fright*, *Stork*, came together with the revaluation of the imperial narrative and the facts of settler origins. Viewed as a cultural marker, there were movies like Peter Weir's *Hanging Rock*, 1975. Weir also did some early work on the emerging music scene, as in his TF Much short film, *Emerging Directions in Australian Music*, featuring Wendy Saddington, the Murtceps and Captain Matchbox, an evocative suggestion of the atmosphere from 1972. *Mad Max*, the big Oz film bang, did not arrive till 1979. Outlaws were revalued in the meantime, not least in the remaking of heroes out of Ned Kelly and his gang, Ned played by Mick Jagger of all people in the 1970 movie of the same name (a surprise, even if his mother was born in Sydney). Cultural cringe was evidently still in play. These were times of transition, of uneven development.

In former times convict lineage was a stigma, spoken of in hushed tones as the convict stain. Now there was a new celebration of local vulgarity, of convictism and the vernacular against the British, as in *The Adventures of Barry McKenzie*, 1972. One aspect of this process, observed by Clinton Walker in *Suburban Songbook*, was the recovery and substitution of local place names for the standard fictional references to the cities of the transatlantic metropoli.[9] It was a time of transition with reference to place names in lyrics. Where did we belong? Billy Thorpe, born in Manchester, living in Melbourne, was writing blues songs like 'Mississippi' – 'I was born in Mississippi/And I saw the river running by …'; local band Mississippi finally changed its name to Little River Band, a more modest local tributary near Geelong, and became a hit in the United States on this nomenclature. It would take another generation before place names drew on Indigenous vocabulary.

So Matt sang:

> You work me so hard that my back's near broke …
>     (We're groaning)
> My brow is wet and my throat's a choke (We're groaning)
> You sent me here for ten long years (We're groaning)
> I miss my whisky and I miss my beers (We're groaning)
>
> Ain't seen a girl since I don't know when
> And the way you treat me I won't see one again
> You broke my head since I spat on a guard
> It don't make me better, it just makes me hard
> Your water stinks cos it comes from a bog
> And the slop you feed us ain't fit for a dog

And the bridge, ascending:

> Well you can beat me
> And try to break me
> But still I spit at you
> You'll never break my spirit
> Even when my body's black and blue …

all this in Matt's unmistakably vernacular drawl, the only dimension of the music that identified it emphatically as Australian.

According to Lobby Loyde, Matt had listened to African-American precedents, perhaps from the Library of Congress. One of Lobby's buzzwords was intense: he liked intensity, the word and the feeling.

> Matt Taylor had an intense way of doing things. I think one of the high markers in Australian recording was 'Black and Blue'. [Its inspiration] was drawn from a Library of Congress copy of a Georgia prison gang recorded on a wire recorder.

It was this old dude, and he's out there, there are two or three hundred guys in this chain gang and they all have big hammers breaking rocks, and this old guy's going 'You break my back, you break my bones' and all the hammers are going 'whack' … Matt took that germ of an idea and wrote 'Black and Blue' … you could put any other pile of musos [in Chain] so long as you had Phil Manning and Matt Taylor, you'd be close; but if you put Little Goose in, then you really got the recipe. But you really need Big Goose in there too … As a combination, it doesn't get any better … I loved them, a great band.[10]

What was the thing about convicts? Modern societies do not always inherit longstanding traditional sources of identity, especially in the so-called new world. They have to manufacture identities, invent new traditions. What they bring with them will not always fit, or work well in these new and distinct environments. The French know who they are over the longer term, though local identities also persist, but they refer to the French Revolution as a myth of origin, and an invented tradition. They must become French, after 1789. Nations are constructed, not least via national cultures, national music, art and literature, later film. The United States has its Revolution, the English 1066; each has emerging national traditions of music and song. White Australia begins with settlement or invasion in 1788, but its origins are in dispossession, harder these days to celebrate, and as a penal colony, also grim. Australia is not born free, but in chains. In the absence of a cleaner myth of origins, Gallipoli is installed later as the imaginary purgatory of blood and iron. Then the ruling culture is anglo, but the subaltern cultures are Irish, Cockney and Indigenous. The dominant anglo culture well into the 1950s still speaks of that convict stain, for many have shameful convict family lineages that go back to 1788; and many cross over with Indigenous peoples, as in other settler colonies.

Into the 60's we witness the slow untangling of a new nationalism. Its features include reversal, as is often the case. What the establishment says, we upturn – now convicts are good, and we are proud of criminalized roots. Convicts, and their bandit heirs like the bushranger Ned Kelly become renewed national heroes; nationalism becomes influential on the left, especially as Maoism. White masculinity is revived as larrikinism, boys looking for trouble, out to bait the cops and anybody else who gets in the way of a good time. And this, of course, spills out into music too, not least in terms of pub rock. 'Nothin to do on a Saturday night /Get into some booze, and maybe a fight' … this was the line registered by the Dingoes in their classic 'Way Out West' in 1973. This represents a masculine culture both at home, and nowhere at home at all. Across the years the boys are back in black, with AC/DC, bad boys for love, with Rose Tattoo, belonging by not belonging, living on a scarred land connected by miles of dirt and cars, and these fantasies spill over into the suburbs too. This is where pub rock emerges into the 70's.

So Australians find themselves in a strange predicament, or else a common one for settler or colonial societies. They are in, if not entirely of, this land, which has been stolen from a people whose presence was denied. They are not English, or American for that matter, though the American dream became increasingly appealing, and elusive, into the 70's, and images of the southern US experience also became influential, though there is never quite any assertive form of Northern or redneck rock here to parallel so-called Southern Rock in the States. But we are still singing English and American songs.

The result is a kind of cognitive dissonance, accelerated by globalization and multiculturalism. This was less immediately a sonic challenge than one of lyrics. As we have observed, Australian lyrics were sometimes comically derivative; named after Mississippi, before Little River Band, born in Mississippi, laying on Arkansas Grass. Some newer, local lyrics and references were brought out by Vietnam, and then 'My Arse is Black with Bourke Street'.

Lobby had nametagged Melbourne in 1967 in 'That's Life', recorded by the earlier Wild Cherries: 'Melbourne is a big big city'– well, bigger than Brisbane; big enough to get lost in, or to lose your girl in. In 'Black and Blue' Chain spoke with an accent closer to Australian, even if contrived as convict, as they had earlier in urban reference, having the blues in nearby Gertrude Street rather than Chicago's Maxwell Street.

Lobby was known to spin a yarn; his nickname, Lobby, referred to this enthusiasm for hustle. He was always up to something, lobbying, organizing stuff, telling stories. But he was close to Matt and Phil, and they all played together at some point, in their home town Brisbane or down south. So this is the story. Matt had a lyric, and Phil had a guitar line. The song had been part of the Chain repertoire for some time, as the bootleg loaned to me by Phil from the Thumpin Tum in 1970 suggests, but longer, looser in rendition, the characteristic components there but in elongated rather than compressed form, and without the finesse, the bridge and the ascending chords. The single format, like 'Golden Miles', brought it all together. But unlike 'I'll Be Gone' or 'Black and Blue', you couldn't really sing along to it, and this made a difference, preserved its musical integrity somehow.

Fifty years is a long time ago. The lyrics now are obviously dated, though there remain audiences of my age who are happy to chant the refrain. One later Chain joke is that they still have a cover band – themselves. The music endures – opening with Matt intoning, floor tom flams and all hands on deck in the studio banging and clanking along on ready-mades, bottles and boxes, making chain-type noises, guitar and bass following the same chords in line like a matched two guitar riff, kind of a 12 bar with the exception that the verse goes up the scale, ascends into the bridge and guitar solo, crisp and note perfect as ever, though not exactly identical to the single version. It was indeed a hit, selling 25,000 copies, an incredible volume for this kind of music at that time. The album hit gold, but over a period of thirty years.

Its cover visuals also date it, though at the time it was a leader. Phil, earlier an art student, recalls that he designed a rough mock-up of what was to follow. The final cover art was done by Ian MacCausland, also then emerging as a leading Australian visual artist for the rock scene.[11] The front cover anonymizes the musicians, by representing their silent and ready instruments alone, each on a kind of surreal blob and tentacle connected umbilically to something located in the distant past … A box of Matt's harps, inert, waiting for the breath of life in different keys, Marine Band at rear, a few chromatics up front, random song notes or set lists thrown in. Little Goose's drums, the grey oyster Gretsch, the cymbals adjusted here slightly to give the image symmetry – ride, crash, splash, heads worn, a sign of experience and duration on the road. Jazz kit set-up, rock sizes, 22″, 14″, 16″. The visual symbols of a jazz drummer – the splash cymbal, those worn heads reminding of a time before stadium rock, giving a different sound to the later super clear resonance of the 90's, a drum sound clean but not clinical, and at first unmic'd. Nylon tips, Regal Tip Combo, more like knitting needles than tree trunks. Phil's red Strat, plectrum under the second fret, sits upright ditto on black background, waiting. Big Goose's Jazz Bass, laminate stripped off, shows the grain of its timber now rather than the original white sheen, lead and strap draped left to right on green balancing against the larger background. The cover is symbolically suggestive. Matt recalls that like the music, the cover may have been conceived under the influence.

> The tubes on the front cover were intended to represent … the music coming together as they played on stage … I used to be fairly stoned when I played in Chain, and I'd actually see the instruments wiggling through each other as I was playing … all the instruments complementing each other, wriggling in and out, not getting into anyone's way.[12]

There was some kind of direction or telos indicated by *Toward*; roots, somewhere embryonic or astrally distant, and allusions to the future. Chain wanted to be linked, between past and future. The instruments, and their absent carriers, suggest both some sense of results and of distance from the origins of the music. At a stretch, maybe there is some suggestion of connection to the possibility of the moonwalk, which as Little Goose observed had coincided with another momentous shift, Big Goose switching to bass. But Chain did not claim exactly to be a blues band. Blues music was something that preceded them, and to which they aspired. They were liminal, somewhere in between.

The cover work of *Toward the Blues* is pleasingly predigital. You can almost see touch of the scalpel or scissors on the papercuts, the slight and necessary imperfection of the designer, the forms cut like the music by hand. The front cover image is echoed in the back, which could be read as a tag or reduction of the fuller front cover image, and on the inside, our actors now revealed, in a spread across the full extent of the cover fold, a little blurry as captured by Jiva, as though he were the joker, always somewhere near the edge of the stage, nearby as they played. Direct sound: no foldbacks; no mixers. There is a kind of proximity, or intimacy suggested in all this. Amps, drums, PA columns at either side of the stage or floor, nothing between the band and the audience at all, no clutter, no hazards of wires or pedalboards or scramble of techies. It is music unmediated by devices or third parties in the contemporary sense. The technologies are put to work, but they do not separate band and crowd. In the audience it is very clear who is leading, yet the experience is close, and shared.

Phil Manning regaled me with stories of repeated fiascos over the cover images. First, the large photo across the inside sleeve was reversed. There are some odd rare copies still around, known by connoisseurs as Lefties. The reversal was corrected in subsequent print runs, and this is the most commonly available inside image across vinyl supplies, as well as taken onto the CD. But second, there was another fiasco with the CD, also recalled. Somebody decided to modify the inside for the CD for the thirtieth anniversary release, replacing Jiva's grainy band pic of the band at full tilt in a gig in a Canberra tent with a black and white image of Sonny Terry and Brownie McGhee; great duo, but no big connect to the album or inspiration for Chain, miles away musically. It was also recalled.

Still, the look of the album cover remains striking. The sound reverberates, as the cover visuals connect us back emblematically to that moment. Toward where? The cover invites, the image of the band suggests, slip out the vinyl, drop it on the deck, volume up, bass up …

If you listen to *Toward the Blues* as it is available on CD today, which you should listen to on cans, there are three additional tracks dropped in for the thirtieth anniversary edition.

'Black and Blue' appears on record in two versions, the single version as well as the track re-laid for the album. These are pretty much note identical with exception of the guitar solo, which Phil here varies. Chain had by now played the song hundreds of times live, and the versions are consistent.

'Judgement' was Chain's second single in this line-up, Matt, Phil, and the Geese. It may be a better song than 'Black and Blue', or at least a better lyric, perhaps more representative of the rock blues style that Chain epitomized:

> I awoke the other night to the strangest sight and sounds (repeat)/The Lord had come in judgement to see if I go up or down/ The only sin that I committed was I joined a four piece band // … Travelled round the country Lord, played in nearly every town (repeat)/ But if I had my whole life over, I would do it all again …

('Judgement' lyrics)

The lyric shifts not only firmly into place, somewhere here, in Australia, but here in time, the recent past, the formative period in the 60's for the musos themselves. There are no convicts here; this was rock autobiography, as in the AC/DC anthem, a *Long Way to the Top* to follow, where rock is almost a vocation, but with a broader metaphysic. Drums syncopate selectively, with emphasis on ride cymbal bell; bass carries the line; Phil lays sharp instrumentation on guitar, riff on wah, top end synced in with Matt's harp. To end it winds down, echoes reminiscent of 'Black and Blue' musically. 'Judgement' may be the best short profile of what Matt and Phil could accomplish together; harp and guitar seem to merge. The two here connect in a similar way to the two Geese. Two plus two is five, or six; the whole is more than the sum of the parts.

'Blow in D' was another taste of Chain live, the wah riff delivered as the basis of extensive improvisation, even as the B side of 'Judgement'. Tentative bass drum strokes build up and thicken as Matt improvises lyrics, doubles time from harp solo to guitar solo, again soaring, accelerating until it comes unstuck, faster and faster and returns to slower rendition of the riff to close, allowing the blow to gently come unstuck.

A song called 'Lightning Ground' seems to have disappeared in the mixes. This was an acid trip song, according to Matt. It was the original B side of 'Black and Blue', uncompromising in its length at 6' 28". Not destined for the Top 40 charts, it had loose lyrics, mountain and fountain, thunder and wonder, dreaming of a new world, but the song follows prog sequencing – four different moves – ostinato, crescendo, rise and fall, beautifully clear instrumentation, bass, drums and guitar, Matt singing over these changes in inflexion, *sans* harp.

Finally, there is 'Gonna Miss You Babe', 1973. This now plays like a small finale, slide and sax, Phil's vocals, edging on funk? bass bops and bounces, pointing in direction of the work that Big Goose was to soon deliver with Renee Geyer on her classic *Ready to Deal* album in 1975. 'Gonna Miss you Babe' kicks along, and Clinton Walker still uses it as a surprise item when he acts as DJ. Timeless? Maybe, or else just fresh, durable, goin' somewhere. Like 'Black and Blue' when young blues roots musos like Josh Teskey and Ash Grunwald remould it live today, recognizing what are now their own roots, fifty years further down that road.

# 3   Before and After: Context

*Toward the Blues* was the classic Chain album, but it also had a history, before and after. The *Toward the Blues* line-up lasted eleven months. Chain's Wikipedia page suggests more than thirty personnel over fifty years. It reads like a who's who of period rock, jazz, and studio players: veteran jazz drummer Graham Morgan, for example, and the almost entire line-up of Healing Force, the finest of period prog bands. This was the thicker culture from which Chain emerged. As follows:

The Chain, Chain or Matt Taylor's Chain members:

- Ace Follington – drums (1968–9)
- Phil Manning – guitar, vocals (1968–74, 1982, 1983–6, 1991, 1995–current)
- Warren Morgan – keyboards, vocals (1968–72)
- Wendy Saddington – vocals (1968–9)
- Murray Wilkins – bass guitar (1968–9)
- Glyn Mason – vocals (1970–2)
- Tim Piper – bass guitar (1969)
- Claude Papesch – organ (1969)
- Barry Harvey – drums (1969–74, 1982, 1983–6, 1988, 1995–current)
- Barry Sullivan – bass guitar (1969–74, 1982, 1983–6)

- Matt Taylor – vocals, harmonica (1970–1, 1982, 1983–6, 1991–2, 1995–current)
- Kevin Murphy – drums (1971)
- Charlie Tumahai – bass guitar (1971)
- Lindsay Wells – lead guitar (1971)
- Laurie Pryor – drums (1971–2)
- Graham Morgan – drums (1972)
- Mal Capewell – saxophone, flute (1973–4)
- Ian Clyne – organ (1973–4)
- George Buford – vocals, harmonica (1973, session musician)
- James Madison – guitar (1973, session musician)
- Mal Logan – keyboards (1974)
- Tony Lunt – drums (1974)
- John Meyer – guitar (1986, 1988, 1991)
- Roy Daniel – bass guitar (1988)
- Bob Fortesque – bass guitar (1991)
- Michael Burn – drums (1991)
- Dirk Du Bois – bass guitar (1991–2, 1995–current)
- Jeff Lang – guitar (1991–2)
- Bob Patient – piano (1991–2)
- Gus Warburton – drums (1991–2)
- Malcolm Eastick – guitar (1992)

Cross-referencing to the *Who's Who of Australian Rock*, we can add Dave Denetar drums, 1988, Mark Greenwood, drums, 1991, and Al Kash, drums, 1988, as well as Trapper Draper on drums from 2016.[1] Chain here is referred to as a perennial blues band;

its own personnel is a who's who. This was a kind of musical chairs, if not also a school of rock, a training ground for a whole generation of musos, or even two. Everybody was playing with everybody else. The Melbourne scene had a kind of intensity of styles, business and personnel that suggest what was special about the moment.

This kind of mobility of personnel is apparent if you check Chain on YouTube for 1971. The best site is *GTK*, for all kinds of 70's rock, blues and prog bands in Australia at the time. What was *GTK*? *GTK* stood for *Get to Know*. It was a source of music intelligence, a ten-minute live show run on the ABC TV channel, the national state provider, initially a creative response to the need for a short filler before the evening news. Public broadcasting, like commercial radio channels, were vital lines of the diffusion of culture. All the same, we may wonder why an experimental rock show on TV? The times, we can suppose; and the demographics, a latent and growing youth audience. What was surprising about *GTK* was that it was consistently imaginative, creative, live, even experimental. Its producers encouraged bands to play versions of the opening theme, a riff by dreamy folksinger Hans Poulson, this way or that, jazz or blues or whatever, and the emphasis was not on the promotion of singles but on non-recorded material. Its logic was not commercial. Screened from 1969 to 1975, it came to be eclipsed by *Countdown*, which was literally Top 40, in a similar manner to the way in which *Ready Steady Go!* was overgrown by *Top of the Pops* in the UK. *GTK* was mainly local, with some global content, Marc Bolan, Led Zeppelin, Steppenwolf, Pete Townshend and Germaine Greer and Lou Reed being grumpy, but mainly local bands live in the studio, jamming or sampling, bands like Chain, Wendy Saddington, Carson, Healing Force.

There are at least three different line-ups of Chain across the period of the immediate influence of the album. *Move*, a commercial TV pop show has the *Toward the Blues* line-up, but miming, and with the guitar solo edited out. Back to 2' 30"! The band looks bored, spaced out over a studio set that somebody thought looked appropriate for a blues band. *GTK* has the *Toward the Blues* line-up for a longish version of 'Booze Is Bad News', Big Goose strumming still like a guitar player, and '32/20' with Kevin Murphy from the Aztecs replacing Little Goose on drums. Goose had already moved on to play avant-garde jazz; Archie Shepp as an inspiration, and a short-lived free form band called Shango was the result, of which there is now no known archival trace. 'Judgement' and 'Munster Blues' on *GTK* has Matt alone from the classic line-up, together with Charlie Tumahai and Lindsay Wells from Healing Force and Kevin Murphy from the Aztecs again on drums. The songs are well delivered, closely rendered but lack the tight elegance of the *Toward the Blues* line-up. Still, these are fascinating clips, allowing us to see the crossover between some of the great locals following the script near perfectly. The procession of musos played with and for each other. Finally, there is a fun/publicity video of 'Judgement', the band goofing around with their roadie, Jiva acting as their besuited agent, engaged simultaneously in moral judgement of the band and ripping them off, leaving the boys with nothing to eat but fish and chips, no fish. Maybe this was why Matt misses his fish, in some live variations of 'Black and Blue'. Likely it is a fair representation of the band's diet at the time. Health giving lentils came later.

On the 'Black and Blue' mime on *Move* Matt plays his harmonica box, as you might mimic harmonica with a cigarette pack. For a laugh. TV was a joke, at least if it were mimed for teenyboppers watching Saturday morning television, stripped of Phil's solo, a cruel cut. Yet it is of course the track which is remembered and memorialized fifty years later, and likely it was an astute business idea to include on the album. Mike Rudd remembers a similar story about the moment in which Spectrum chose for artistic reasons to leave their period anthem 'I'll Be Gone' off their first album. Result? No sale. Single sold, LP not. This was the spirit of the times for hippie musicians. They were never in it only for the money. Zappa was clever, but wrong.

This was the period in Australian rock history when venues were shifting from clubs to pubs, and certainly from singles to albums. The really big sales albums were yet to come, Skyhooks and Daddy Cool. Studio albums ruled, but the rough edge of live albums was also pervasive, epitomized in the reign of Thorpie – Billy Thorpe and the Aztecs. Thorpe generated several live albums, later, all with some degree of chaos, but exited his Chicago blues style period with an album bizarrely called *The Hoax Is Over*, where Lobby and the Pig shine, but self-indulgence and play acting or pretence prevail. They were all stoned, falling over stoned.

*Chain Live* was a different kind of live. The first Chain album was recorded live at Caesar's Palace in King's Cross, the red light district of Sydney in July 1970. Chain was a house band here, often playing alongside a band called L'Affaire and its knockout vocalist Kerrie Biddell, sometimes supporting Biddell when need arose. So here they record live, but this is live in the club, not the pub or stadium or park. Small at this stage was still beautiful. The line-up and sound are significantly different from *Toward the Blues*. This is a five piece, Phil and the Geese together with Warren Morgan on keys and Glyn Mason on second guitar and vocals. All tunes are originals. There is some banter, including a tag from the band as Ignazio and the

Silvertops, riffing on 'Never on a Sunday', from the Chordettes, 1954. Five tracks, this was also radical for its time; closer to jazz, and with prog motifs steered by Warren Morgan, aka the Pig, aka Warren the Organ Morgan, again classically trained but here constrained by the limits of the period tool of the Hohner Clavinet, which struggles to carry the weight of the music. The Clavinet, like its popular portable alternative, the little Farfisa organ, was not built for edge. It had none of the presence of its big sister, the Hammond B3; and the B3, built originally as a church organ in the mid-30's, had projection and presence in the room but was harder to find in Australia, where musical instrument supplies could be short, as well as a serious challenge to carry or transport, and the gospel tradition had none of the routine presence it had in the southern states. Every church hall in the south of the United States had a Hammond; in the secular culture of Australia, where religion was less completely dominant in everyday life, the bulky keyboards were harder to find. The Clavinet was another thing altogether. It was not a piano, but technically a clavichord. It lacked the touch, finally, of the Fender Rhodes, also hard to beg, buy or steal in Australia in this time. But you could buy a Hohner for $200, about $2,000 in contemporary equivalents, and it fit under your arm. Drums were always a bigger physical challenge, but Chain had their single roadie, Jiva, who also did the photo for inside the album cover for *Toward the Blues* and, as a note on that cover observed, helped keep the band supplied.

As for *Live Chain*, Little Goose here syncopates kick drum throughout. Drums and bass are close, but so are bass guitar and bass drum. The vocal, featuring Glyn, drops in and out. Phil told me that the band spent more on the dope bill than on the recording costs for this session – $62 on drugs, $30 on recording (multiply by ten these days). You can hear it, on both accounts. The album was taped onto a two-track Revox A 77 machine. The opening track is 'Pilgrimage', an earlier train song intro carried by sloshing hi hats, with symphonic arrangements from the Pig. Track two is the original 'Black and White', before 'Black and Blue', carried by Phil on the clean and then syrupy tones of the Gibson Stereo 345 that was then his main guitar. 4/4, drum solo, again led by time on ride cymbal opening out onto the whole kit. Walking bass, tumbling bridge, returning to the clean chords of the Wes Montgomery octaves, rim tapping keeping time on snare, alternating with double time frenzy. Track three is 'The World Is Waiting', which is an elegiac, heavily arranged prog rock piece, using the period twin guitar lines held together by the bass riff. This is followed by 'Gertrude Street Blues', a sad, slow, wailing lament by Phil about a band visit, Phil as driver, to the venereal disease clinic in said location, then a tough part of the city, now at the peak of its gentrification process fifty years on; 2022 *Time Out* has it as the second 'coolest street in the world'. Bass drum syncopates throughout. The rhythm is based on the kick back. The closing track, 'Chaser', opens with the tag of 'Roll Out the Barrel', jokes abundant, strong prog lines, measured arrangements, drums picking out accents, highs and lows, fast and slow movements culminating in a spill or free for all; they all go crazy, sort of.

There was another kind of chaser, or coda, to *Live Chain*, which has since surfaced on the internet. These are the so-called *Armstrong Sessions*, recorded at Bill Armstrong's studio, not in Sydney but in the old butter factory in South Melbourne. Three tracks run for fifteen minutes. First is Warren's love song, 'Betsy', also a name for Phil's Gibson Stereo, which soars throughout. Second up is 'Ain't Got Time For Nobody', and third an alternative version of 'Pilgrimage'. Glyn carries the vocal, the five-piece line-up from 1970. As elsewhere in these more formative days, there is a strong soul influence, echoes of the Band. Soul was a stream to run right through in this work, later for example on Phil's tingling version of Percy Sledge, 'When A Man Loves a Woman', on the 1978 album *Manning*, using the Phil Manning Stereo that Maton built for him, and sold in small release. It sounds, and looks, like the Les Paul Professional that Lobby christened George Guitar, modelled after Jan Akkerman's Framus, and though it was dual jack, wired for stereo, Phil does not recall using it that way. Who carried a split guitar lead? The Phil Manning Stereo became a collectors' item; the West Australian writer Tim Winton told me he had his under the spare bed, awaiting a possible change of medium in later life should the need or desire arise.

There are some other traces of the period available on bootleg. Phil Manning offered to lend me a CD, made off a cassette tape by his guitarist mate Greg 'Sleepy' Lawrie (Sleepy?, another nickname, he liked to play with this eyes closed). It runs for one hour twenty minutes, and successfully conveys the atmosphere of the live gig as I remember them. The experience of listening back for me, after fifty years, was a bit like peeking out from behind the curtain with a massive time delay. Sleepy ran the cassette tape at the Thumpin Tum around October 1970; there are jokes about the impending Melbourne Cup, held in November. The tape, if not the gig, opens with a longer version of 'Black and Blue', in formation, about seven minutes, and without the nifty turnaround of the later versions, but tougher, closer maybe to the mood of the live blues they then played. This is followed by a song called 'Early', a version of 'Early in the Morning' with Phil on vocals, and then a lost classic: 'My Arse Is Black with Bourke Street', the band's anti-Vietnam war, pro Moratorium song, a boompa, following the

Elmore James model but with entirely local lyrics. Next is 'No Tears', a three piece – Matt steps aside – drum fills, paradiddles, crescendos, culminating with harmonica re-entering late and a cymbal solo; ending, as often the case, with a tag. Next up is a sweet, slow version of the BB King standard 'Sweet Little Angel'; featuring the Gibson Stereo and Warren's Hohner, which at slow pace, low volume, can actually here be heard, bass guitar and Hohner stepped in unison. This was a signature live song for the five-piece line-up, which can be heard on Barry Harvey's' Music Texts *Reverbnation* site, fab balance and power played up loud at 6'.02". A glimpse also appears in vignette on the movie *Once Around the Sun*, which features a number of period bands who played at the Ourimbah Festival in January 1970, including the Aztecs with Lobby, Wendy Saddington, Max Merritt, Copperwine. 'Pilgrimage', a festival song off *Live Chain*, follows, on Sleepy's cassette; 'You're Wrong' and 'Snatch' to close.

Meantime, amidst this radical earnestness of white boys playing the blues, or something heading in that direction, there were still bills to be paid, rent and food, and other stuff. Rock music may be a way of life, but it also involves making a living. Chain and their more musically accomplished mates did session work, backups, jingles, even TV work including in Phil's case the children's talent show *Young Talent Time*. Evidently their considerable skill sets were continuing to expand; and little wonder they were attracted to the silliness of the tag, the light banter of being on stage, and the funny side of showbiz. Music would always include comedy. Like earlier, classic figures in the Black blues tradition, they would play anything. Music was special, but it was also how you made a living. They were literate and imaginative, tight and disciplined, could read charts and respond to instruction, and it all paid a lot better than gigs in dive bars. The band's weeklies might be $150. Phil remembers something like a session rate of $AUD 110, ten times that amount converted to today's value. Average weekly earnings in Australia were a little over $100 per week in these times. So sessions were good money. A few dates like this and you were rich for a week. Phil and Big Goose, especially, played on some of the key tracks of the period of awakening into the 70's. It's a long list, beginning with Rob EG, ending with John Paul Young, for whom the Pig (Warren Morgan) became musical director. In between, they backed Wendy Saddington, Kerry Biddell, Alison MacCallum, Russell Morris, Dutch Tilders, Renee Geyer, Tina Arena, Vanessa Amorosi (live), even the vocal crooner Kamahl with full orchestra when he needed guitar backup to complement those schmaltzy strings.

The quality of the backup was high. For a good period taste of the quality of the blues cut, c. 1972, try Dutch Tilders's version of Jimmy Reed's 'Wee Wee Baby' from his self-named album. The core backup by Chain bounces the song along. Further musical highlights from these sessions include work with Russell Morris, on the 1971 album *Bloodstone*, most notably on the hit single 'Sweet Love', the period kind of slow love song that late goes into double time for solo fills. Phil provides the hot licks. Another period classic is Saddington's 1971 'Looking through a Window', a song written by Warren Morgan, credited to Warren and Billy and featuring the matching and crossing guitars of Billy Thorpe and Manning. Manning's is the sweeter. The song is moving, plaintive and beautiful, but almost disappears under a massive string arrangement and Thorpie's antics, the thunder of those Link Wray power chords, and the late obligatory change to double time. These antics came to a head at the Melbourne Town Hall Concert 1971, which included Chain and Carson, and a monstrous phallic plastic blow-up stage set which went berserk, prompting a longer than usual drum solo as the techies went into damage control. Chain, as usual, just played, held the line. They did humour, but not paranoia. The showmanship is musical; this is not entertainment, in the sense of amusement. It's not simply music for pleasure, or boys with their toys.

Forty years later Russell Morris returns himself singing the blues, on *Sharkmouth*, 2012, and other albums to follow. His latest album is symptomatic: it is called *Black and Blue Heart* (2019). Saddington's life spun out in other ways, but the blues record in Australia was changed by her presence and the live time she spent with bands like Chain, Company Caine and Copperwine. As Julie Rickwood shows in her analysis of Wendy Saddington and Copperwine Live – 1971 – in *An Anthology of Australian Albums*, it is, like '*Live Chain*', direct to disc, warts and all.[2] It carries the atmosphere of its moment, live at the Wallacia Festival, and like *Toward the Blues*, it can chill to the bone, Russell Smith cutting it on the Les Paul Goldtop.

So then there was *Toward the Blues*, self-disciplined and tight, self-constituted in comparison: the musicians stoned but tight as Little Goose's snare as Chain, on their own turf. Then, there was *Live Again*, recorded again at TCS in October 1972. This was the result of contractual obligation. Phil Manning tells me the recording process lacked direction, compounded by the absence of a wilful producer. The line-up was as for *Chain Live*, Phil, Pig, the Geese and Glyn Mason. This album, again live in the studio, also had six tracks. It opened with 'Take Your Time', which the band did, at 11'41". It's a spritely prog jam, with maybe eight different sequences, crescendos and falls, multiple time changes, octave chords and wah from Phil, and the panoramic depth of Pig relaxed on an acoustic piano. This is followed by 'Pig's Blues', another lament about longhairs being different in a conservative culture, and being moved on, this with a kind of Fats Domino barrelhouse feel. Drums are dominant, with a really busy bass drum and jazz fills laced over the top. Third was 'Seventeen', a tag or joke at 1'14". Opening side two is 'The World Is a Rocky Impression', another marathon coming in at 13'.15", with up to ten sequences. A crisp drum solo tumbles across the speakers into piano solo, fortissimo, then freak, and finally a transition back to rock and roll vocals. This may be the best available Chain profile of Pig and the jazz energy of the band, though there is another ballpark indication on *GTK* in 1972. 'Betsy' is a 3/4 ballad that doubles into 4/4 for piano solo, Little Goose using brushes, even: not only rock and roll, at 5'.48". Back to *Live Again*, 'Mr President', indicates the cultural influence of Americanism still, but also reflects the prominence of the United States via the strategic alliance that took Australia into Vietnam in the first place. 'Mr President' is a great tune, thick and rich, a groove with strong solos from Phil and Pig, bass and drum thick and solid. 'Leaving' takes a smirk at 'Black and Blue', and offers Phil's period ecological lyrics – can't stand your pollution, leaving the city etc. Glyn Mason's vocals and guitar echo his contribution to the earlier live album, offering a kind of glue to bind the others together. The small audience apparent from their noises off suggest something of a party in the studio, which it was.

*Two of a Kind* was a more transcendent moment, Gudinski licensing a confabulous combination of Chicago blues, on one side of the album, with a single track 'How to Set Fire to an Elephant', prog let loose on the other. Muddy Waters and band were touring Melbourne at the time. Chain was the support. The musos got on well. They spent time together, talking, drinking, killing all that time waiting to play. Phil remembers

Pee Wee Madison waking him up, banging on his hotel room door on tour too late at night, playing him a new song standing in the corridor. 'Phil, listen to this! We have to play this!' The song was his own, 'Two of a Kind', which in clever pun became the album title and symbolic staple for such different yet parallel musical processes.

Biracial bands or sessions were rare in Australia. The demographics are different. In the United States, the precedents were the Paul Butterfield Band and differently Booker T and the MG's, and the 1969 album by Muddy Waters, *Fathers and Sons*, followed by further collaboration between Muddy and Johnny Winter as producer, Leon Russell and the Kings. Earlier there were the Rising Sons. Then there was the breaking experience of Jimi Hendrix Experience, biracial and transatlantic. The Australian demographics and histories of race were different to the United States, and the Indigenous relation to popular music here was more apparent in country and western, later rap, reggae and hip hop. In this period there were more notable Maori presences in the blues scene, including Reno Tehei, Leo de Castro, Phil Key, and especially the legendary Charlie Tumahai, who played in Chain after 1971 and appears on that *GTK* clip of Chain's 'Judgement'. Black Allan Moarywaalla Barker, a Yindjibardi man from Port Hedland in WA was active in the eastern states across this period, fronting whatever white pickup band was on the bill. He was a minstrel, who like Wendy Saddington, would be supported by whichever blues band was in the house for the night. Barker left a fine album called 'Fire Burning', from 1983, whose lyrics indeed remind us of Robert Johnson's 'Hellhound'. Blues was led earlier by women like Georgia Lee, who recorded the first Indigenous or mixed race female blues album – the first blues album, *The Blues from Down Under* – in Sydney in

1962. Lee combined the blues tradition with the vernacular, covering 'Beale St Blues' but adding 'Yarra River Blues', after Melbourne's main waterway, which until the 80's was the proverbial city river, the city with its back to it, facing away.[3] She was preceded by white blues women like Joan Bilceaux, who was active in Melbourne from the 30's, earlier in the Croydon Merrymakers, then covering 'Basin St Blues', working with Louis Armstrong and Bob Hope, and ending up in TV, Channel Seven's Melbourne Hit Parade and with a show called *Blues Studio One* – all this in the 50's, when the rest of us were glued to Doris Day.

These kinds of blues performances took place in clubs, cabaret, and coffee shops, more rarely on TV or radio. In the 60's blues was most often manifest as acoustic, folk, or else as rhythm and blues, evident even in rock bands like the Easybeats, whose first single 'For My Woman' had a so-called jungle beat in 1965, and whose hit 'Wedding Ring', same year, offered the girl of Stevie Wright's dreams the seductive alternative, 'crazy music/ Or sing the blues.' Brisbane bands like the Purple Hearts featured various blues songs, not least via the Paul Butterfield repertoire or Graham Bond. The Masters Apprentices in Adelaide did not follow the standard blues songlist, but their name spoke to its importance: they saw themselves as the apprentices to those who led the way from the Delta to Chicago, Muddy, for them Bo Diddley, Jimmy Reed, even here on the other side of the earth, in the antipodes. Adderley Smith, named after a local city street, worked in Melbourne, featuring the harmonica honk of Broderick Smith. Sydney led with Phil Jones and the Unknown Blues, whose orientation was more to the Delta than to Chicago. Later in Sydney the Foreday Riders rocked on, featuring the lilting harp work of Jeff King. Harmonica was popular – portable, cheap, yet capable of all the presence of the

Memphis saxophone once jammed against a mike. Little Walter had initiated a small revolution of his own, the things you could do with a harp and the reverb control on a personal amp. By the 70's the unlicensed club scene had exploded, particularly in Melbourne, and then the pub scene. It took a while for the nuance of the harp away from the PA to set in. House PAs were crap, built for sermons or, as the initials suggested, public address, council meetings, not for rock music.

Chain stretched across these periods and venues, but they were really a club combo. Their manager into 1971 was that young man called Gudinski, who offered them so much work they would also be groaning. As the cliché has it, you learn a lot playing three spots a night six nights a week, whether in Melbourne or at the Reeperbahn. One of Gudinski's great contributions to the Australian rock scene was to support local and overseas blues, recording WA bands like Sid Rumpo, then Carson and managing Chain as well as supporting prog bands like Mackenzie Theory. Gudinski developed a network that took in schools and dances and became something close to a monopoly in time. He also brought to Australia leading overseas players such as Willie Dixon, Freddie King, Hound Dog Taylor, Alexis Korner, Sonny Terry and Brownie McGee, and Duster Bennett. We gobbled all this up, alongside BB King, Buddy and Junior, Osibisa, Mahavishnu … it was as though a hundred doors had opened, in the club scene, around the traps, on vinyl and on *GTK*.

Some of the best in music or creation occurs as the result of accident. Putting the members of Chain in proximity with the younger members of the Muddy Waters band was a brilliant move, intentional or nay. Next thing you know, they are playing together. The first side of *Two of a Kind* opened with Pee Wee Madison's new song, followed by three standards: 'Reconsider Baby', 'Everybody Has to Lose Sometime' and 'Blues with a Feeling'. Phil plays behind Pee Wee and Mojo Buford, on harp, the whole held together by the vice-like clamp between the Geese. 'How to Set Fire to an Elephant' is another thing altogether. It features an extended Chain line-up, with Mal Capewell on reeds, Sleepy on second guitar alongside Phil, and Ian Clyne, another ex-jazz player from Red Onions and cult 60's band The Loved Ones on keys on the tune that he wrote, together with the core of the Geese. There is an extended drum solo, which goes through the mixer with some strange psychedelic effects, echo and reverb. By this stage, according to Phil, Little Goose has his own PA made up by Vase from Brisbane. His kit has also grown, two floor toms and the timbales, sizzle on the ride cymbal. So the drum sound is fuller, some of the patterns closer to ostinato, and a step beyond the straighter combo drumming on *Toward the Blues*. It is a fascinating experiment in pushing into prog, jazz rock fusion. These days we would likely prefer to listen to it clean, without that added distortion.

*Straight as a Die* (1973) was a brilliant moment, Chain presented as Matt Taylor's thing, or the other way around. Its hallmark period song 'I Remember When I Was Young', was excluded, however, once more from the album. Again, a conceptual approach to the music overpowered the commercial logic of maximizing sales. Chain were not interested in making money. Matt, the hippie, likely found the very idea offensive. The album was Matt's and the songs were expressive of his way of life at the peak of his hippie or commune phase. But the band is Chain, the *Toward the Blues* line-up, with Sleepy added in again. It was recorded live outdoors on the Kingston Park farm Matt was renting outside Frankston, a bayside suburb, then more rural, now suburban, solar heating panels as far as the eye can see. The album opens with a hymn to 'Mother Nature', all rock, little acoustic on the whole album (a Krishna dance, and a loose blues with Sleepy now on Dobro resonator guitar). 'Mother Nature' is a salutary reminder of how strong the argument for ecological consciousness was becoming in the years that unfolded after the 60's. We all became ecologically conscious. This was a bit like the hippie version of Marcuse's *One Dimensional Man*.[4] If the world was becoming total, or totalitarian, it might be time to step out, to start over elsewhere:

> All we need is a place to stay/Food to eat but not too much everyday /Love and friendship from the people we know/ But if you think about mother nature /Then you better start right now!
>
> *(Straight as a Die* album)

More:

> We were churned out of high school
> And made to go to work
> Got a new set of values
> But in us freedom lurked
> If this is reality
> Or so we are told
> Look into your mind
> And the truth will unfold …

And then the punchline:

> We work hard for possessions /Thinking wealth is happiness/ But there's no satisfaction being involved in such a mess/ That shiny new car will only last five years /But you can forget anything with icecold beers …

All we need is a place to stay /Food to eat but not too much
everyday … love and friendship from the people we know/
If you think about mother Nature then you really gotta act
right now!

This kind of message hit us hard around 1971, and in the years
that followed. We were reading *Brave New World* and *1984* as
part of the year 12 curriculum to cheer us up, expecting the
worst, having earlier watched *The War Game*, now reading
the *Pentagon Papers*; and we were eligible to be conscripted
to fight in Vietnam until December 1972. This kind of dialectic
seemed entirely possible: one wing of the state was warning us
we were emerging into totalitarian futures, the other getting
ready to train us up for combat. The more you thought about
it, the worse it got – factory food, factory fodder, the prospect
of endless, pointless work, a rising war machine, generalized
conformism, older people who would gratuitously abuse you
on the street.

Music, in all this, seemed like a lifeline. It seemed to carry
hope, or at least to keep a window open to some small utopia.
Matt's was an advocacy of the period hippie sensibility – to
show by example: live simply, so that all may simply live. It
all pointed in the direction of tuning in and dropping out.
Farming. Vegetables. Track Two of *Straight as a Die*, 'Brisbane
to Beechworth', follows Matt's own path from up north to the
commune in regional Victoria which was then to lead to years
spent on a commune with commune leaders the Robinsons
in Western Australia, before his return to the city life of gigs
and pubs with the later band Western Flyer. 'Simple Decision'
was another exhortation, the imperative to change the world
by alternative living now. 'We'll Never Do the Same Again' was
more the story of remission, repentance, hope for resurrection,
in the face of impending apocalypse; the world has stopped,

nothing is working, even the pubs are closed, food and petrol gone: Save us, if you please! 'What's the use of living if you can't find an escape?' Sorry sorry! we will never ruin the planet again.'Chickens' was a high point, a political attack on fast food and factory food production. It is pointed at Kentucky Fried Chicken, which had arrived in Sydney in 1968 and together with McDonald's transformed its suburban skyline, and waistline, with the ubiquitous presence of the Golden Arches and that sweet Southern gentleman smiling all the way to the bank. We all became vegetarians.

'Chickens are not normal/they'd have intercourse if they were normal/they only live so we can give our money to Colonel Sanders …'. 'Hall of Fame' was a loping blues, double stroke snare and timbales from Little Goose, Big Goose bubbling on bass, Phil and Sleepy crossing guitar lines, Matt's drawling vocals lambasting the very idea of celebrity, chromatic harp blues floating over. 'Krishna Loves You Too', was a response to the local street presence of Hare Krishna driven by those Geese to 7′.16″, and 'Dance', the closing track, was exactly what they did on the streets of Melbourne, harp and tabla mingled together.

The anthem, however, is 'I Remember When I Was Young': not included on the album. A good way to sell a single, perhaps, but not the album, which can still be found around the retro shops in its pristine McCausland rural, romantic detail artwork, now evocative less of space-time than of Walter Crane or art nouveau.

> Well I remember when I was young and the world had just
> begun and I was happy
> I used to wonder about the earth and how it moved around
> sun so snappy
> Imagination growin wild makes a very backward child

Before and After: Context

> Or so they told me
> So back at school I just sit around waiting for the sound so I
>     could go home ('I Remember when I was Young')

… and play vinyl. Playground stuff, the stuff of childhood, to tricks on bikes, early unrequited loves and killing time at school until 'growing up meant you get to fly a Sabre jet and fight a few wars' – life straight out of a 50's, Korean war, comic book, but then music arrived to save us …

> Well I remember when I was young the Beatles turned me
>     on I really blew my mind/
> Then I heard the black man's blues they really blew a fuse in
>     ma head/
> So with some friends we made a stand and formed our own
>     blues band it was a real good thing … ('I Remember
>     when I was Young')

Matt's lyrics are more carefree and yet more poignant and personal than the other Chain candidate for an anthem, 'Black and Blue'. The song doesn't really work as a singalong, though you can often see punters mouthing the title words at a gig. They are keen to remember when they were young, like the rest of us, and would like to go back there. Those lyrics are nostalgic enough to resonate still with the experience of the crowd, and to endure. They register the fact of the British Rock invasion, and the retrospective discovery of the lineages of the blues back to the source in the Delta, as the dominant narrative or myth had it.[5] 'I Remember' also had a bop style, a kind of medium lope or shuffle, but at a pace that was in sympathy with the cheerful nostalgia of the lyrics. The album and its music also appeal to that moment of rediscovery of the bush as utopia, where the call of the simple life beckoned blues folks locally as it had for Alan Wilson, Canned Heat and others, as exemplified in the United States and widely followed here in 'Goin' Up the Country' (1968), which even the Beatles were listening to for *Let It Be*.[6] It was time to leave the city, if you had a car; those distances were long, after all, in Australia, and you would still need electricity to plug in the stereo, and the fridge. As Phil sang earlier, you could exit with a suitcase in your hand, on pilgrimage; or later, after Sunbury, just get out, leave behind that 'City Life', as he sang, escape, start over.

But just as some of the major actors on the scene locally and globally were about to head out to the country, to the local or imagined version of the Big Pink, rock music here swerved into the suburbs. The famous venues for bands like Chain were the city clubs like the Thumpin Tum, Sebastians, Catcher, Traffik. Then came the pubs, the Whitehorse, Doncaster Inn, Village Green, the Chevron or South Side Six, and larger venues like the Melbourne Town Hall for big bang events like the Aztecs in 1972. Then there were Festivals, from Mulwala, Myponga, Launching Place, Ourimbah etc. and the game changer, Sunbury, from 1972 to 1975.[7] Much lauded and widely promoted as the Australian Woodstock, or even 'bigger than Woodstock', Sunbury was in fact different. The cultures were different, and already the moment was different. It lacked the more effusively hippie atmosphere of Woodstock, and the variety and fame of its celebrity line-up. The line-up here was largely male, with little of the light relief or diversity as in Sha Na Na at Woodstock, except for Captain Matchbox, 'the loudest jug band in the world'. But again, it was ours, all local, suggesting something of the musical nationalism or sense of self-sufficiency in the air – who needs Deep Purple and the revolving door of overseas celebrities when you can have the Aztecs even louder, and able to connect with the crowd? And there was prog involved, as in Wild Cherries, Co

Caine, Spectrum, Healing Force and Chain. The risk was that the experiment of music would become drowned in a sea of booze and a different code of misconduct.

'Booze Is Bad News' never stopped Chain from drinking, but 'I miss my whiskey and I miss my beer' now gave way to the new popular chant: 'suck more piss', the charming image indicating the physical cycle: liquids in, liquids out. White Australian culture born pickled in alcohol; rum was its earliest currency. What was at issue here was whether Sunbury was a music event or a big piss up. Clearly there were elements of both. Michael Chugg, an old mate of Phil's from Launceston who had become a leading promoter, remembered that the mood of Sunbury after a spell felt like the Nuremburg Nazi Rallies. It was scary, into the night, fires were burning, wire fences, and it was time to go; he had a car, and was able to escape. Missed the action, and the atmosphere. It was time not to flee the city but to take refuge in it, at home again.

Phil Manning suggested thirty years later, after the rise and fall of the festivals, 'It was a time when the hippie thing was declining and the drunken afternoons of too much beer, sun and basic rock developed. The music went from being experimental to being moronic entertainment for yobbos.'[8]

Billy Thorpe was then king of the kids. He spent a life in music as entertainment, giving the people what they wanted. Now he took charge. Thorpie was still confident, all those years later:

> I was reading an article where Phil Manning, who is a wonderful guitar player but just missed the point, was saying that most of us who believed Sunbury was the beginning of the music scene, he believed that it was the end because it turned into endless riffing by morons for yobbos … I mean,

Phil, that was the charm! But what happened was it scared
the living shit out of 95 percent of the industry.[9]

These were ominous signs of a scene shifting into spectacle
and tribalism. Since when was fear a driver of rock music?
Was this just more macho bravado, shocking the bourgeoisie,
frightening the Establishment? What did this leave for those
who hoped that the audience would listen, rather than behave
badly? Plainly hippie culture was on the skids. Die hippie die!
Better to stay home with the stereo up loud. As Ian Port says of
the electric rupture in his book *The Birth of Loud*, talking here of
Dylan at Newport, 'Volume, after all, is power'.[10] Certainly it was
some kind of elixir for the Aztecs. Staying at home, at least, we
could turn Chain up, or down, even off, go outside, lie on the
grass, watch the clouds scud by.

Phil Manning saw Sunbury as some kind of epitaph for
gentler days. 'That whole aspect of the alcohol fuelled crowd
basically brought music back to the level of sport. And sport is
fine but music is an art form'.[11] As Matt sang, 'That shiny new
car will only last 5 years/But you can forget anything with ice
cold beers'. For Chain and its culture, 'suck more piss' entailed
the risk of becoming part of the problem, boofheads, rather
than the possible solution or alternative. This new culture
of Oz rock, as pub rock, was no place for head music, or for
its gentler practitioners. As for the intelligent alternative, it
was to resurface with the sarcastic glam of Skyhooks and
the sharp guitar-edged doo-wop of Daddy Cool. The mood
was changing, as the 70's consolidated, beckoning to the
80's. The moment of *Toward the Blues* was passing. Small is
beautiful was giving way to something else. Rock music was
in danger of becoming a blood sport. Club rock was giving
way to pub rock. Bigger venues, much more volume, heavy

drinking right through rather than before the gig; this was another scene to the world Chain had entered just a few years earlier, a different configuration of music and masculinity.

Local gangs like the sharpies made a sport of assaulting longhairs. The boys were back in town whether for pub rock or for glam, though the girls were also making it new, not least with local initiatives to follow, like girls only Rock 'n' Roll High School via the impetus of Stephanie Bourke. Angus Young and AC/DC went global and ballistic, but Chrissie Amphlett and the Divinyls took over in Melbourne. In later years, my American students presumed Chrissie was American. Maybe she was channelling Wendy Saddington, rather than Chrissie Hynde. In any case, the rock world was also becoming shinier, more given to glam and approaching the revolution of MTV, where the visuals would begin to overshadow the sonics. 'Black and Blue', in any case, was broadcast in black and white. Like that classic photography, it endures, stretching across generations and the worlds of everyday life as well as placing it into that distance.

# **4** Time and Place: Big Context

What was the moment of Chain? What was the national and global context in which *Toward the Blues* emerged? What was Australia, into the 1970s? Like other such places, Australia is a collective noun for an aggregate of cities, regions and country, formally united at the federal level, but still colonial and often divided in different ways. It has ironies of its own. As George Seddon observed, it is a small country connected by big distances, a relatively small population clustered mainly around the fertile crescent, and large expanses of desert or arid land in between.[1]

Its dominant culture, since British invasion in 1788, is Anglo, colonial, in engagement with the environs and its original inhabitants, then Anglo American into the twentieth century, and multicultural. Australia is a new-world nation-state based on dispossession, on the founding myth of *terra nullius*, and on a political and legal tradition known as White Australia. Its roots in convictism still resonate, not least in the English imagination. It is a culture based on a hunger for land, gold, money and now real estate. Its nineteenth-century utopia included the hope of democracy, and maybe equality for white men, even votes for women. Into the twentieth century, its innovative legal institutions, such as industrial arbitration and the living wage, made it something of a world leader, in aspiration at least. Today, after the latest round of globalization, its dynamics are as much governed by the rat's wheel of endless growth and acquisition as any other like nation. Social acceleration rules, even if we have no collective idea of where we are going. As the writer Michelle de Kretser acidly puts it in her novel *Scary Monsters*, our core values now are no longer democracy or equality, however conceived, but rather home improvement and household debt.[2] She is joking, of course; or not.

This is a useful tic, as it serves to highlight not only the blissful tsunami of consumerism that dominates everyday life, but also to draw attention to our suburban chase. Dominated by cities like Melbourne and Sydney, Australia is at the same time a place where everyday life is lived out in the suburbs, and this is bound to affect the patterns of culture and especially rock music, in both sonics and lyrics. Rock music in Australia may be expected to carry suburban inflections, as well as the marks of British culture early and later, after the Beatles. Then there are American influences well into the twentieth century and especially after the Second World War, in the Age of the American Alliance that came along with Fordism, Hollywood and rock and roll, the Korean and then the Vietnam War.

As Seddon observes of Australia, this may be a strange combination: small, with big distances. Nothing quite like the UK or the United States, the major musical and cultural influences until recently. This will also have serious effects on rock music and its distribution. Small population, long distances, lots of driving, in dubious vehicles, and accidents earlier on, then flying. Into the 70's musos were still dying or maimed by road accidents, including Little Goose's break of his right hand. Stewie Speers, drummer for Max Merritt and the Meteors and also a jazz drummer, was crippled, Max disfigured in a gig drive accident, Bob Birtles left limping. Adelaide band Zoot almost died in a major crash. The rock life was dangerous; asleep at the wheel was no joke.

There was more critical mass in the big cities, more gigs and musos, and some serious 'fuck you' innovation in the smaller, where the rules were less clear, this alongside small-town indifference and endless demand for Top Forty or singalong. In the suburbs, there were some wacky venues, ice rinks, church and civic halls, school halls, sometimes town halls, and, of course, sheds and garages. Into the 70's, rock music moves into public hotels, and this signals a big shift from Oz rock, as it is retrospectively called, to pub rock – beer barns, ear-splitting volume and toxic alcohol consumption, turning, as Phil Manning put it, the art of music into a sport. Chain, indeed, worked across the period of the transition from club and dance culture to pub rock. They were in this sense decidedly old school, in sympathy with the taste of prog rock, which was understood by its followers as head music. If you were in the room, you were supposed to listen. No cell phones.

Clinton Walker's work on Oz Rock tracks this transition, from what he earlier called the *Inner City Sound*. Walker then was writing about punk and after in the later period, 1976–85, though his more recent classic is *Suburban Songbook – Writing Hits in Post-war/Pre-Countdown Australia*. *Countdown*, the colour ABC pop and rock show 1974–85, serves as an icon of Australian rock in a similar way to Sunbury, the emblematic rock festival that ran annually in hot summers across 1972–5.[3] Other trends can be discerned, including a 70's into 80's shift into inner suburbia, anticipating gentrification, in places like Carlton and Prahran. These developments can be traced across several recent anthologies, *Boogie*, from 2012, *Silver Roads* and *When the Sun Sets Over Carlton*, both released by Festival Records in 2014, and the earlier compilation of music from the *Go! Show* on TV in the 60's. But before there was punk or Oz rock there was sound from the suburbs, from rock and roll in the town halls of Heidelberg, Preston, Coburg and Ringwood and it continued, as those suburbs still continue to house the majority of the Australian population and sustain their everyday lives. The population of inner city Melbourne remains modest, around 170,000. But in the time of Chain there was live music regularly, nightly in the city.

There is some good literature on the earlier and formative moments of Australian rock. David Johnson has a great book called *The Music Goes Round My Head*; Ian Marks and Iain McIntyre wrote a fine book, *Wild about You*. More generally, there is the work of Ed Nimmervoll, one of the great period rock journalists, *Friday on My Mind*. Most encyclopaedic is David Nichols's *Dig*, the text so rich with detail that it threatens to collapse under the weight of its own data.[4] On the Western Australian scene, there is an amazing dossier by Murray Grace and John Mills called *Jive, Twist and Stomp: WA Rock and Roll Bands of the Fifties and Sixties*, which makes it abundantly clear, again, how many of our eastern hero players came from the west.[5] Then there is Aotearoa/New Zealand. The rule of thumb is that a third of Australian musos come from NZ including Max Merritt, Mike Rudd, half of Healing Force, La De Das, Dragon, later the Finns – Split Enz, Crowded House etc. Here there are great studies on this scene by Jon Dix, *Stranded in Paradise*, and Chris Bourke, *Blue Smoke*.[6] Much of this material works by way of dossier, reproducing details, names and recording schedules, featuring both words and visuals. For narrative or stronger interpretation, some of the best work includes that of Clinton Walker, Jon Stratton and Craig Horne, as in *Roots* and his study of Spectrum, *I'll Be Gone*.[7]

Rock remains a vital part of everyday life, but less so of scholarly interest. So how best to tell those stories? The point is not that rock moved from the city to the suburbs; it was always present in both, following the larger demographic. Its forms may have been different in city and suburbs. Into the 70's, the time of Chain, it was located in the CBD and connected into the 'burbs by a network of venues. The inner city venues then declined, to be replaced by beer barns; but there was always an inner city or city ring art scene, as in the Tote Hotel in Collingwood; still there: the famous sticky carpet.

The common picture of Australia into the 70's was celebrated by intellectuals like Hugh Stretton, who saw the suburbs as a place to flourish, and indeed rock bands did.[8] Its critics saw Australia suburban settlement as the kiss of death for creativity; their secret models of the good society were London and Manhattan, later maybe Stockholm or Berlin. Australian population, in contrast, was taken to be dispersed, small, derivative of Anglo culture. But how small? In 1971, the moment of *Toward the Blues,* there were 13 million souls, half what the population is today. The demography was mixed, then and now, the significant differences after 1975 including Vietnamese refugees, Asian and South Asian then African. The dominant proportion of the population remains Anglo, and its dominant cultural forms are also Anglo, but leavened by the other (I remember sitting in with a Greek blues band in the 90's; these days world music is everywhere, though the inner city scene is yet to recover from Covid).

The 70's in Australia were ruptural, or at least it felt like that. Whitlam the modernizer abolished conscription and the White Australia policy, offered different social democratic horizons, and anticipated the shift towards multiculturalism and globalization. It was a key moment in the transition to a new modernity, and to the cultural forms that would dominate the next generation of cultural production.[9] A new cultural nationalism was apparent, even if everyday life and music was still dominated by cities, and especially by the scene in Melbourne. The structure of city life prevailed.

Six major cities, state capitals, plus the national capital Canberra, spread across the continent. Industry historically in the south east, mining extraction north and west. This would suggest some significant regionalism in music and everyday life. Surf music was bigger in Sydney, where there is more surf, country music dispersed throughout. Adelaide was a major impulse to the development of rock music, and later Aboriginal music, and a feeder to other capitals, especially Melbourne, which dominated the club and dance scene into the 60's. In Melbourne in the 60's and 70's, there were networks of youth gangs with strong tastes in music and fashion. Sharpies were sometimes taken for skinheads, versus mods and then hippies, the first two in different ways snappy dressers, mods especially present in Adelaide, where there were significant numbers of British migrants around model cities or new towns such as Elizabeth, named, still, after the Queen, but home to driving rock bands like Cold Chisel and the Angels. Adelaide was the centre of demand for the visit of Beatles in 1964; the smaller city was originally left off the tour list, but public demand proved sufficient to secure the Beatles stop by. It was also the area where Robert Stigwood grew up, in Port Pirie, a bit like Nick Cave, from a small Victorian wheatbelt town called Warracknabeal. Punk had featured especially in Brisbane, exemplified by the Saints. Indigenous musos were best connected to country and western, as travelling troubadors, then later to rap, hip hop and reggae. The rock breaker here was Yothu Yindi, and their anthem 'Treaty'.

What was Melbourne into the 70's, then? Historically it was a gold city, Marvellous Melbourne, made rich by the rushes of the 1850s, dominated by Victorian architecture reminiscent of Manchester until the skyscrapers arrived.[10] Its public face was conservative, establishment, male dominated and stodgy; but like others such, it had an underside, a wild side, a massive network of gigs, 160 per week? inner and outer, clubs and dance halls and church and civic venues into the 1960s.

Inner city Melbourne was bluestone, rock venues in Victorian terrace houses, clubs with even Victorian names like Sebastian's and Bertie's, or in warehouses, The Thumpin Tum, Traffik, Catcher, halls like Ormond and then TF Much. The pattern of growth for live music continued into the present century, as Craig Horne claims. By 2017 Melbourne had 553 live music venues, in contrast to 453 in New York, 385 in Tokyo and 245 in London.[11] These numbers sound boosterist, or at least enthusiastic, but if the rough contrast is at all valid it speaks loudly. The rock image of Melbourne came to be goth-inflected, dressed in black, obsessed with coffee culture, and inclined often to stay indoors – the weather in caricature like the north of England in winter, the results good for music, stuck inside. Why not play, or listen? Music, or canoodling, might also keep you warm. The grim alternative was contact sports; Melbourne is also the home of Australian Rules Football.

As a Marxist might ask, so much for the superstructure, what about the base? What is the economy that holds all this up? Gold, wool, extraction dominated the political economy of Australia from the nineteenth century; in Melbourne, banking. Australia was late to develop manufacturing or import substitution. No Detroit or Dagenham, no Motown here, no Great Migration in the American style. For automobiles, it was coachmaking, then assembly, then local manufacture with limited export opportunity. Housing and all its auxiliaries follow, engineering, roads and bridges, including later consumer goods like TVs and musical instruments – import substitution – with two leading exemplars, Maton guitars and Drouyn drums, and big amp stacks in the style of Marshalls, including local brands like Strauss and Vase. For rock music is also a mode of production: its instruments, technologies, records, even merchandise, fashion, its own modes of consumption. There was the usual kind of cottage industry and DIY. When desirable guitars like Fenders were hard to secure into the 60's, thanks to import restrictions, some aspiring musos would set to making their own, sometimes with hilarious visual effects, klutzy cardboard cut-out templates, self-made oddities resembling lamb chops or space probes as much as they did guitars.

Folks were indeed adaptive, and quick to respond to metropolitan rhythms with what Clinton Walker conversationally calls creative mimesis. A good story here involves New Zealand band the Chants RnB, including Mike Rudd covering 'I'm Your Witchdoctor' by Mayall with Clapton 1965, within weeks of its London release. We were listening to the 1967 Mayall/Butterfield EP within weeks of its London release in 1967, again. Local musos were hungry for overseas product, but this does not mean that they duplicated what they could get their hands on. Mimesis is additive; even when musos look to copy, they generate something new. Art school R n B was part of this culture, again like the UK. Into the 70's and 80's, campus venues proliferated. The expansion of the university sector meant that colleges became a vital site for venues and the transformation of music culture, as student union fees became a momentarily reliable source of budget that musos could garner for day gigs on campus, evening gigs and rave ups in union halls. As elsewhere in the empire, there was a generative connection to the worlds of the art school, Dada and surrealism, the Goons, Zappa, dada, drugs, sex and generalized mayhem, even radical politics. This was a hot breeding ground for prog rock.

What was prog? Progressive rock came to be the name given to a category of non-standard, orchestral, jazz and blues influenced music dominated by bands like King Crimson, Yes, Soft Machine, Nice, ELP, Genesis, Pink Floyd. These were the big acts. The apogee of the form was arguably in smaller, less popular more vanguard bands like Nucleus, from London, *Elastic Rock*, 1970. There was some explicit crossover with blues, as in the early Jethro Tull, Blodwyn Pig, the Allman Brothers in 'Elizabeth Reed' or 'Hot Lanta'. Often English, prog was also American in the case of the Allmans, where the giveaway was two drummers – one rock, one jazz, playing sweetly together, alongside guitar duets and keyboards. This set a pattern for Tedeschi Trucks to follow, though the multiple drummers trick went back at least to James Brown. King Crimson got up to three, which is too much, though it makes the point. Excess! Impact! Variation! Themes, movements, doubling, surprises: prog was structurally similar to jazz in form, verse, chorus, solos each in turn, but often more choreographed than openly improvised.

The genre was by no means only English, however. For then there were the Mothers of Invention, Zappa in a category all his own. And 1971 was a big year for Zappa fans, producers and consumers alike, with the arrival of his own live Fillmore album, prog plus ruthless sarcasm elevated into an art form. Miles away musically, there was in the United States Chicago, or Blood Sweat and Tears, jazz rock with some distant echoes of earlier big bands. Here the rock combo plus brass section added in some idiosyncrasies in composition – Erik Satie? but in the case of Chicago, supercharged by the fierce guitar work of Terry Kath. For the year 1971 the global killer for prog would be the Mahavishnu Orchestra with *The Inner Mounting Flame* – there you go, a combo with the pretence of an *Orchestra* – but nothing like Sun Ra, rather smallish, disciplined and impossibly clever, each muso better than the last, as with 'Dance of the Maya', which lurches into the blues at what counts like a 20/4. And there we were, copying Mahavishnu after our own manner in high school in 1971. We did not, however, copy Chain. We may have hoped to be like them, but they were the real thing, and here, ours, local. So with Chain, we listened, learned and talked. With Mahavishnu, who visited in 1974, we gawked. McLaughlin was everything live he was on record, and more; and then there was Luc Ponty, Ralph Humphrey and Michael Walden. These guys took prog out the door.

On consideration, and in retrospect, prog as a category may have been situational. Prog was more progressive in the sense that it represented progress beyond the Chuck Berry formula, the staple of rock through to the Stones, or Jimmy Reed or the Elmore James 12 bar. Logically it might be taken to stand less for the idea of progress than for that of complexity and unpredictability. You can't sing along with prog, which often has no words – it's all sonics, all instrumental, or ever be quite ready for the next clever tricks and near impossible to follow time signatures. Shock and surprise were the motifs built to impress. Prog was built on the showmanship of the virtuoso, typically classically trained and with preferences well into jazz. Prog was wow music, music for musos. Chain was all this and more, the simplicity of blues and sophistication of jazz and prog all thrown in together.

Was this culture in Australia then mimetic? derivative? imperial? governed by the tyranny of distance? isolated, doomed to be vernacular, or populist? Not all institutions or cultural practices in Australia followed British precedents. The

Australian Labor Party was formed before the British Labour Party, and was as heavily influenced by local factors as any others, including the centrality of itinerant and agricultural labour before the development of manufacturing industry. Little wonder then that country music mattered. This in contrast, for example, to the Australian Broadcasting Commission, more clearly derivative of its model in the BBC, with innovative exceptions like *GTK*. *GTK* was one of those moments when nobody older was steering, nobody was watching from above, and the younger folks like Ric Birch took the wheel. So while the overseas influences in Australian culture were clear, there was also significant cultural traffic, and innovation. The biggest Australian rock band in world after the Wiggles, of course, was AC/DC. This was a long way from the toothy lyrics of the Gibb Brothers – more British migrants – which took a more novel turn with 'Spicks and Specks' in 1966. More interesting was what you might call the hybrid culture of Oz rock. Migrant, British often, but with something local and different added. AC/DC's 'Long Way to the Top', 1974, remains symptomatic: Chuck Berry with bagpipes, its famous video version performed on the back of a flatbed truck travelling up Swanston St in Melbourne. The Youngs were a family story, of migration and cultural transmission, from George in the Easybeats, to Malcolm and Angus, and Vanda/Young as the writing team with a long tail. Peculiarly local? Colonial, at least: old world meets new world. Something new results.

Then there was also cultural reflux, or the reverse of this mimesis, when peripheral songs showed up in the culture of the centres. As mentioned, Manfred Mann covered 'Black and Blue'. This was likely the result of a shared bill at Beatty Park Pool in Perth in 1971. The International Blues Rock Festival featured Chain as well as Deep Purple, Free, and Manfred Mann, all in the most Australian setting of a swimming pool, chlorine and concrete – heavy. Phil was friends with Mick Rogers from way back, when Mick was in Procession, who left behind astonishing records like *Live at Sebastian's* from 1968 before disappearing into London's Marquee. In 1972, Long John Baldry covered Daddy Cool's 'Come Back Again' in league with Rod Stewart and Elton John. In 1973, Bowie covered 'Friday on My Mind', the first of many to do so. Rod also featured with Sydney band Python Lee Jackson on 'In a Broken Dream', recorded in London in 1972. The larger flows of cultural traffic were from the centres out; the daily and weekly circuits of antipodean rock music circulated more widely internally than out. And like the Easybeats, bands headed out for fame, or like Normie Rowe, to record with Jimmy Page and John Paul Jones as session players. The rest of us stayed home. Some, like Normie, were then shipped out to Vietnam.

The 70's in Australia are often thought to be a period of cultural flourishing and democratization of culture (and democratization cuts both ways, as de Tocqueville had anticipated). Film, writing, fashion, music; Whitlam. Whitlam was the closest we had to Trudeau *pere* – sophisticated, urbane, cosmopolitan. But he was also divisive. There were serious social divisions over the Vietnam War, but also over what might be called the emerging split between the new Australia and the old. There had been seriously divisive moments in white Australian history, from the Frontier Wars and massacres to the Great Strikes of the 1890s, the First World War and battles over conscription, the hard days of the Depression, the split between Communism and catholicism in the 50's and the Vietnam War into the 60's. Enthusiasms for multiculturalism, as elsewhere, also come together with its reaction, in the form of revived White or Paranoid Nationalism. Local struggles in recent times parallel and draw inspiration from MeToo and Black Lives Matter but also draw on a long tradition of struggles for Indigenous rights and the rights of women, the former combined with white willingness to tolerate black deaths in custody.

The experience of the Vietnam War was central to Australian society into the 1970s. It became a kind of rallying point. Vietnam was, after all, nearby: Australians were coming to grips with the idea that they lived in Asia, where the European Far East was rather our Near North. More, the issues raised by the war were simultaneously international and local. The connecting tissue was the conscription by ballot of young men to fight and die in Vietnam. Vietnam brought the revolution home. Revolution was a period metaphor, and it echoed in the world of vinyl – 45, 33; revolutions were vinyl cycles as well as metaphorical ruptures, real or imaginary. Wendy Saddington had a band called Revolution. Soon there was an alternative rock newspaper called *Revolution*, from 1970–1, *High Times*, 1971–2 and another called *The Digger* from 1973–5. Lobby Loyde even edited a paper called *Daily Planet*, part of the Mushroom Empire. Leftwing sects and parties like the Communist Party grew, the antiwar movement providing fruitful fields for recruitment. Moratoria were not just the easy 'Revolution' of the Beatles, politics in song. Rather, in cities like Melbourne, there was a confluence of radical politics and rock music. Trotskyism, Maoism and the Viet NLF were all mixed up with the music of Chain and Spectrum at antiwar demonstrations.

How did we get our music in the 70's? Australia was late with TV, 1956, but then there was *Bandstand*, in black and white, with various rock and pop shows through to *Countdown*, in colour. Even the former Prime Minister, Gorton, was captured in 1975 doorstop on film saying he couldn't talk, had to rush home to watch *Countdown*. This was popular, but not camp, as in Aotearoa/New Zealand, where ex-conservative PM Muldoon actually took on a part in the *Rocky Horror Show*, as MC, in garters. But it was suggestive of movement, of something in the water. Rock was popular, and was now even a Sunday night family event.

Early rock included Johnny O' Keefe, the local Wild One of the early rock scene, and the more sedate Little Pattie, cousin of Chrissie Amphlett, later made famous as the schoolgirl pouter of Divinyls, female echo to Angus Young as schoolboy with a Gibson SG. Around Croydon, where I grew up into the 60's, there were rockers and jazzers, Beatles wannabes – mods and stylists – and R n B Anglos. In Sydney, migrant hostels like Villawood brought together the personnel for bands like the Easybeats. There were clusters of R n B bands across the cities. There was a blues story before the 60's, but for my generation white blues came first, in terms of reception, and it came on vinyl in response to British invasion after the Beatles and what followed: soul in the case of PP Arnold, Chris Farlowe and The Who: Roger Daltrey singing James Brown, blues via skiffle. As George Harrison said, according to Billy Bragg, there would have been no Beatles without the blues: the Beatles took you back to Lonnie Johnson, who took you back to Leadbelly. So there were coffee lounges, and skiffle, and jugbands. It was a while before the Beatles laid down 'Yer Blues' in 1968; and blues could always, as with McCartney, be recognized more readily as the path pioneered by the Roosters, whether in Clapton's band's rendition or the Stones version of the hit 'Lil Red Rooster' in 1965.

First up, likely, for the big cultural blues bang was John Mayall and Beano, as the Clapton Bluesbreakers album of 1966 was known for its cover image, the God Clapton reading a local comic book. Certainly this is the big bang Phil remembers. Tony Worsley, his velvet swooned bandleader, brought home a copy from Adelaide. My brother came home shaken the day he heard the first, trashcan Fleetwood Mac album blasted out of big speakers facing onto the street in a city store, an old trick pioneered earlier in Chicago by labels like Chess. Peter Green was the virtuoso, but Jeremy Spencer really had his way with us; we were all trying to sound like Elmore James. Then there were the Hendrix early albums, then the regress, going back to discover the roots. And the weird of first and second albums by the white guys, Cream, Heat, Led Zeppelin, flipping over from gentler to ferocious, this apparently resulting from a synergistic combination of volume and drugs. Hendrix may have softened from his first album to the second, or at least his recipe had. But there was always 'Voodoo Chile', to follow 'Red House', and there was always 'Killing Floor'. There was psychedelia, as well as the blues.

What were the supply lines for this kind of music? Where did this music come from? Global, and local; vinyl, print media and oral in its sources, but without the long generations of transmission characteristic of the classical example, in the United States. You could go into the city for music supplies, and we did, travelling in from the suburbs on the train. But there was also stuff in the 'burbs. An English migrant called John Robinson established a music store in the Arndale shopping centre in Croydon, mimicking the UK experience severally. Arndales were the first American malls in the UK. JRs had drums, guitars, amps, Rose Music, Yamaha and Marshall plus strings, sticks, heads and upstairs spaces to jam, plus records on vinyl. Sheet music – you could buy 'Black and Blue' on charts via Festival, embellished with a nicely posed shot of the band outdoors looking longhaired and blue, all for forty cents, appended with the clear instructions to get the mood right: 'Slowly, heavy beat'. At Croydon Market you could buy Levis and Raybans, or ripoffs, but also serious supplies of blues music. There was a guy who had a stall selling Pye and Astor, but also some great American labels – Verve, Vanguard, Elektra, American small labels that covered wild music from Zappa to Jimmy Smith. There were classics, like Leadbelly, Sonny and Brownie, Elmo, transitional white figures like Tom Rush, John Hammond Jr and Koerner Ray and Glover. There were anthologies including later UK collections like *Blues Anytime*, 1968, Page and Clapton grating together, Dave and Jo Ann Kelly; *What's Shakin'* with Butterfield, Clapton and Winwood. There were other markets like this at Camberwell and elsewhere in the 'burbs. Ian Collard and Benny Peters, of the contemporary Melbourne blues band Three Kings, tell the story on stage that they independently discovered the blues, and especially Jimmy Reed, in this way.

We had some British schoolmates, kids whose families had migrated to Australia under the postwar Anglo support scheme; Keep Australia British. My brother Fred, our later bass player, began to play tea chest bass with his schoolmates, David Hubbard, later to croon for Captain Matchbox, and the brothers Bruce and Lin Knapp, the latter English migrants who had arrived in Melbourne clutching cheap semi-acoustic guitars – were they Framus? like Hofners? singles by the Who and Pink Floyd before they became megalo ('See Emily Play'). In fourth form a cockney kid, Richard Towe, joined us at Croydon High School, wearing longhair and a furcoat, looking for trouble with those tough boys who didn't like boys who looked like girls. There were fistfights, elicited by us playing *Disraeli Gears* over the School PA at lunch. Rubbish! Wimps! Chris Finnen, our English migrant guitarist in school, was nicknamed Hendrix for both visual and sonic reasons. As well as the wannabe Afro and the clothes, he carried a Dutch Egmond guitar which we managed also to loop through the school PA. Finnen became a stalwart of Australian blues, playing independently and together with Matt and Phil, most recently in Matt Taylor's Chain in 2021.[12]

Other avant-garde music came via our school friend Vivian Lees, soon to become the leading entrepreneur behind the music festival Big Day Out into the 90's. Our musical world exploded. There were all these amazing albums: Ten Years After, Fleetwood Mac, Taste, Butterfield, Mayall, Chicken Shack, Winter, and all these anthologies. There were papers, *Melody Maker* and *NME*, and magazines like *Downbeat*. When I asked Phil Manning how he picked up that banjo string on E trick from Clapton, he told me he read it in the music press. There were other sources of intel well before the internet. Locally, there was *Go Set*, which always had the What's On or gig guide, and *GTK*; and there was always the radio, including ABC for jazz and solid commercial stations, 3 UZ and then 3 XY, also given to organizing concerts for youth and to promoting longshot singles like 'Black and Blue'. Then we discovered world of live, clubs and discos. There was an older art scene, jazz, Red Onions, folk clubs, acoustic blues with stars like Margaret Roadknight, Danny Spooner and Dutch Tilders. This was an older scene, where the pickup, the clipon and the acoustic guitar, often the Eston with one inbuilt lightweight pickup arrived, plugged into whatever amplification came to hand.

The really revolutionary change in this musical story, in Australia and elsewhere, was the wider production and distribution of the electric guitar, and then its serious amplification. You could do a lot with a Vox AC 30, but the bigger boxes delivered exponentially more. Lobby's finale gig, under chemo featured ten Marshall stacks. Chain was never given to this kind of overkill; though it was Lobby's last gasp, and half the boxes may well have been empty, but made the point. That point remains: the central technology of white blues was the electric guitar and serious amplification. That's not an amp – this is an amp!! The broader effects were also manifest. For harp, looking for trouble, you could hear it in Little Walter: reverb, miked through an amp rather than the PA, reverb control so important to the generation like Peter Green that followed Hank Marvin on guitar, and then to the mixing desk and the promise of balance. Deep Purple: Jon Lord, Hammond plus Marshalls. Dylan after Newport! Mike Bloomfield behind him. Electrification was transformative, even if it was also to become something of a monster across time.

Small music combos hitherto were acoustic, or nearly, dominated by brass, trumpet, Miles, sax, Coltrane, piano, Brubeck, vibes, Milt Jackson – hot and cool, respectively, reigned hitherto. Charlie Christian pioneered amplification in bigger bands or orchestras, where acoustic guitar could not be heard for the brass section in the 30's. The development of the solid body was another ballgame: Gibson, Fender, Bigsby, Gretsch, Guild and the jangling Rickenbacker semi-acoustic, still hollow bodied.[13] For Fender, there was the integrated guitar and amp set-up, mirrored in the design of the Fender Rhodes piano, modular and snug in fit, amp underneath. The recipe made in heaven was Fender plus Marshall, the transatlantic combo identified with Hendrix. Volume, feedback, reverb, tremolo and later, pedals. The best global exemplar, along with Jimi, was Jeff Beck, who came to treat the Stratocaster in particular as a tool, a machine for making noise, sonics and mimicry, a quantum leap beyond the Spanish guitar. Sometimes the Strat was referred to as the guitar from Mars – futurama, future designed, yet also taking a decade waiting before the radicals worked out what they could do with it. Feedback became a virtue, and an experiment in control, noise became something to work with, potentially to master.

The central figure or guitar hero in the Australian scene was Lobby Loyde, from his early days, Fender Jaguar and Vox AC 30 through to Les Paul and Marshall, though almost all significant rock bands or prog bands were guitar based or dominant. The best samples are GOD, on *GTK* 1971, and the longer, more fully expressive version on *Summer Jam*, 1973. Lobby and Phil had always been mates. Lobby may in fact have been the biggest single influence on Phil, not least, as Phil remembers, on his tremolo technique. They met on the day of Phil's arrival on the mainland in 1965, at a rehearsal studio in Camberwell where Lobby was rehearsing with the Purple Hearts, Phil had come to join the Blue Jays. A younger Phil decorated Lobby's legendary Fender Jaguar, the Yellow Canary. But if Lobby went to loose and loud licks, Phil went for precision and sympathy.

The most powerful exception to the guitar hegemony in Oz prog would have been the band called Tully, dominated by the power Hammond, the extensive drum set of Robert Taylor, then bass guitar; then later, the Moog synthesizer. It's an interesting point to remember: no digital currents yet in the mainstream into the 70's. Tully may have been the Australian exemplar of high prog. Their self-named album, *Tully*, Live at Sydney Town Hall 1969–70 had one track per side, at twenty and thirty-two minutes, respectively. This project emerged from a keen collaboration with composer Peter Sculthorpe and a mixed collaboration, less universally keen with the Sydney Symphony Orchestra, music described by

Tully organist Michael Carlos as an odd mix of Vanilla Fudge and Coltrane. Trippy head music, indeed.

With a rockier edge, as well as sarcastic wit, there was Spectrum. A concert-based band with long and open-ended sequential arrangements, their Plan A format was to lead to a Plan B; same line-up, light equipment, lighter material, Hammond traded for Hohner, called Murtceps, Spectrum in reverse: they would play two sets in a row, one in each format. The snappy unit Ariel was to follow later on. Rudd often strummed guitar, open handed, following the earlier pattern of the Loved Ones. Then came the heavier note players, led by virtuoso Doug Ford in Masters Apprentices, crossover R n B and prog, as in 'Rio de Camero', same year: 1971. There were heavy guitarists like Kevin Borich, lateral players like Ross Hannaford, various bands like Bakery, Friends, McKenzie Theory, Fraternity, Co Caine, Tamam Shud, Kahvas Jute, Ayers Rock, and Sebastian Hardie differently offering instrumental walls of sound dominated by guitar, often moderated by Hammond or brass, sax or flute, but held together by loud sustained guitar. In rock, the trend peaked with AC/DC, the Young brothers band, where that second guitar was as central as the first. The form was even celebrated by Stevie Wright in 'Guitar Band', another Vanda and Young song looking to be an anthem.

But if guitar ruled, it was not the only fruit. Not only the Hammond bands, but also bands like Syrius, the Hungarian prog/jazz band sans guitar that visited Australia and stayed awhile, not too easy before the Wall came down, and leaving the legacy of Jackie Orzacsky – all on record on *GTK* in 1971. It was as though a hundred musical flowers had bloomed. This was the culture that Chain developed and blossomed in, emblematic part to the whole.

And it was a culture, not just a moment, a thick scene of musos, ideas, styles and vinyl. These were players who lived together, and lived to play. As maverick harp player Brod Smith remembers:

> Carson County I had found out (before joining) were part of the Chain camp of professional musicians who I knew and liked as players … I found out that Chain and Carson were heavily into Canned Heat … For a while Barry 'Big Goose' Sullivan played bass and Mal Logan joined in on keyboards.[14]

Brod Smith lists various personnel crossovers. Meating was another iteration, including Matt performing 'Bad Luck Feeling' together with Big Goose and Mal Logan. Big Goose went on to Flite with Leo de Castro etc. They all lived together, first in Carlisle Street, St Kilda; they knew each other's repertoires. They were musically promiscuous, and their personnel was in constant flux. All this guided by the young Gudinski, as much a fan as an entrepreneur of this local blues rock boom, and then was mixed in with the direct influence of the masters, like Muddy, when they came to tour and to share.

For an aural sample, there is the anthology, *Golden Miles – Australian Progressive Rock 1969–1974* (Raven). The most representative song of the period and form was indeed 'Golden Miles', a 1971 pop song at a carefully measured 3'. 25", octaves of guitar, swirling, heavy Hammond, Charlie Tumahai bass and vocals crisp and perfect, drums understated, guitar less dominant if not subordinate. For 1971, the local hero of prog, rock and guitar would have been Lobby. Phil Manning, by contrast, was in and of team, the journeyman, not the hero; his game cricket, not football. Yet as you take in 'Booze Is Bad News', the power of his solo guitar is chilling, and you know you are in the presence of harmonic greatness, something reaching towards the blues, but also towards the cosmos.

So what was in the mix? There were prog elements in Chain's *Toward the Blues*, along with jazz proficiency, playing blues forms with prog influences, all connected by the riff. The culture emerged from experimentation within the frame of blues and prog, a scene rich in resources, human and musical, local and global, a certain level of technological sophistication together with a remaining simplicity of tricks, a direct connection with the audience live or on vinyl. The strong inclination to improv was only possible on the basis of the elective affinities between Big Goose and Little Goose, and Matt and Phil, and these two pairs in combination=combo. With this double loop in musical geometry two by two was more than four. There was familiarity, and sympathy. Melbourne became the forcefield, though the bands and their members often came from elsewhere across Australia and the Tasman. Sometimes the stars aligned, as in September 1971. Their technical moment mattered, electric yet relatively unmediated by devices, on the cusp of the super amplification that also came to be its own undoing. They shared the right skill sets and material, aided by substances that were enabling rather than disabling. Maybe, finally, Phil was right when it came to the rock scene. Booze came, after all, to be bad news. But there were also larger, cosmic forces at work. As Greg Macainsh observes of the specificity of that moment, it had an intimacy or proximity which was to be erased by the new wave of globalization, accompanied by the civic privatism that went with the rise of electronic music.[15] If you could play it by yourself in your bedroom, why go out and share the space of those dirty little clubs? That was the scene of *Toward the Blues*. It was small-scale, communal and alive.

Albert Collins, the Master of the Telecaster is reputed to have said to Matt, 'God, you guys are playing blues like it ain't no blues I've ever heard before!'.[16] Later in life Matt began to call the genre Oz indigo.[17] Not blues, in the strict sense, but somewhere out there in that ether, a close but marginally distinct atmosphere, ineffable in itself, and best carried by the music and its lyrics rather than words on the page. So then, for us all, it is time to move on.

Chain moved on, alone and together. Matt and Phil became the core pivot of various further musical expeditions across the five decades to follow. The Geese became known as stalwart session and touring players into the new century, sometimes together as Brother Goose. *Toward the Blues* became an icon of this formative moment of Oz rock, or whatever it is best called; white blues, after the British, like blue-eyed soul? Antipodean blues? Oz blues? Oz indigo?

'As I look back I swear it was a good good time': Matt varied those lyrics to 'Booze Is Bad News'. Even when he was still young, he remembered when he was younger. The year of Chain in its classic line-up was a peak experience, for them and for those of us hanging round Melbourne in 1971. Go to the window! or, head for the deck, plug in those cans! and travel across time, towards the blues, closer to the sun.

# 5   Back Pages

## *Personnel

Who were Chain? There were various line-ups, as we have seen, four key musos in the classic line-up that delivered *Toward the Blues*. We know more about Matt and Phil, under the spots, and with more interview data; less about especially Big Goose, who died of rock-related disease in 2003 and was less given to talking, and rather less about Little Goose, who was also quiet and has retired from active musical life, back home in Brisbane.

Matt Taylor was born in Spring Hill, a suburb of Brisbane in 1948. Here we have the benefit of an autobiography, *I Remember When I Was Young*. Like Phil, early triggers were the Beatles and Stones, but then the harder edge of Chicago blues came into play, and harmonica became the key vehicle for its expression. Sources included US record shops with jukebox remnants like Jimmy Reed. Butterfield was a big influence across this scene. Matt frequented the Red Orb in Fortitude Valley, where Matt learned from Lobby when passing through, sitting in front of his amp, fetching his drinks. Lobby and Matt played with the Geese at the Orb as Wild Cherries, Phil also passing through. Matt came to Melbourne to play with Bay City Union in 1966, moving onto bands like Meating, Horse and Genesis with Greg Lawrie. Chain was a peak, as in *Toward the Blues*, but Matt also became an earnest follower of theosophy and then the alternative life of the counterculture, as manifest on *Straight as a Die*. He took up communal living in Victoria, then Western Australia. He later formed Western Flyer, after a long spell of the alternative life in Balingup in WA with the alternative tribe of the Robinsons. Details of this life after *Toward the Blues* can be found in various net interviews looking back, but especially in that valuable memoir/autobiography, *I Remember When I Was Young*, delivered together with Phil Riseborough and Toby Burrows, High Voltage Publishing, 2021. This is a fabulous document, rich with detail, memory and images, and clearly indicative that for Matt 1971 was just a beginning. The book functions as a general resource book for the earlier period, scrap book, diary, social history and all. It shows something of Matt's centrality to the story of Oz blues. Gudinski called him King of the Blues in Australia, following Muddy in the United States. Matt came to refer to the form as Oz Indigo, in the ether of the blues, but toward. You can hear this latter version on his Oz Indigo suite of albums, *Catalyst* (2018); *The Prize* (2020), and *Excited* (2021).

Phil Manning was born in Devonport in Tasmania in 1948. He was trained in piano from age 6 till 14, and took up guitar at 15. He discovered blues in magazines, then the Beatles and did the regress thing. His father was a radio electrician, helping build his first amplifier. At 17 he started art school in Hobart. There he found a key music dealer, a folk singer with a stock of blues albums, Bill Hicks. Now he was into Robert Johnson and Leadbelly, with white rock and pop always in the mix. He came to Melbourne in 1966, aged 19, to fill the guitar spot vacated by Vince Melouney in Tony Worsley and the Blue Jays. Worsley had further stimulants, including a copy of the Clapton Beano album. On arrival he went to rehearsal studios in suburban Camberwell and met Lobby Loyde, who was rehearsing there with the Purple Hearts. This began a lifelong friendship. He used Lobby's Warrior 240-watt Strauss amp on *Toward the Blues,* and decorated Lobby's famous Fender Jaguar with its yellow livery and blues heroes' references. So he was much inspired by, but so different to Lobby, who had also been classically trained but had the anarchist spirit in him after those early days of R n B. The next chapter was Bay City Union, Chicago blues with Matt Taylor, and a ripping single, 'Mo'reen' backed with 'Mary Mary', Nesmith via Butterfield. Phil played with the Laurie Allen Revue with the rhythm section of Daddy Cool and headed WA to join Beat'n Tracks, then travelling back to Melbourne after winning the Battle of Sounds there. Then there were the various iterations of Chain, first of all when Beat'n Tracks picked up with Wendy Saddington. But there was also a life outside and alongside Chain, followed by and coextensive with other projects like Band of Talabene, Phil and Pig (Warren Morgan) as Pilgrimage, then Mighty Mouse, Chain again, Manning, and a solo life, which can be sampled on *Phil Manning: The Essential Acoustic Collection* (2006). Interviewed recently in *The Senior*, Phil claims there is no such thing as getting old, only experienced, like the blues classics such as Muddy who were already old when Chain played with him and his band in Australia fifty years ago.[1] Playing these days better than ever, with more emphasis on new songs and acoustic and less on the very loud, he says he can't believe how fortunate his life has been, playing music for a living. As with the rest of the band, *Toward the Blues* was just a beginning; there was a whole life to follow. See most recently his self-sufficient album *Out of My Shed* (2021).

Barry Harvey (Little Goose) was born in 1950 in Brisbane. Barry learned drums and piano from age 7, as well as double bass. In the early choice between piano and drums there was no competition. But familiarity with piano meant that he had a lifelong relationship to music with piano as its core instrument. He began working on what was to become his Berklee book at 13. Barry was the local wonder boy, gigging from the age of 11, able to read and also unionized, signed up by his father and thus able to work in licensed joints, cabarets, concerts and other venues. He saw Joe Morello, a key moment, with Dave Brubeck in Brisbane in 1962. He played with Phil and Big Goose, and Lobby and Big Goose at Red Orb. He revived piano at Berklee College of Music in Boston in the 80's for arranging, acknowledging the centrality of those eighty-eight keys. Little Goose returned to his planned book, and Australia in 1982. After Chain he played with Flite, with Leo de Castro, with Big Goose or Harry Brus on bass, then later the brilliant Dirk du Bois, who replaced Big Goose in Chain after his death. He also played with prog rocker Rob Mackenzie, later touring with Kevin Borich. Goose taught for twenty years privately, and in private schools. His book, which he began at age 13, was finally published in 1994 as *Polyrhythms – The Text of Music Phrase: Fully Written Drum Set Charts*, *Sight Reading and Phrasing for All Instruments*, Fairfield, Queensland, 240 pp, and can be accessed in hard copy at the National Library of Australia, 781.221 H341. You need to see this book to believe it – awash in dense notations, handy hints, good vibes and intricate detail. It is a work of obsession with drums and their role in music. See also Amanda Dweck, 'Chain and the Night Man Walked on the Moon' *Toorak Times* 29 December 2017, as well as 28 December and 30 December issues, and see the public radio interview with John Broughton, Casey Radio, 97.7 FM, listed 8.6 2018 (2004). Salut, LG!

Barry Sullivan (Big Goose), Brisbane, 1946 – 27 October 2003. Brod Smith remembers from early encounters that Big Goose was highly creative, but that he was also seriously disciplined, like Dingoes bassist John du Bois and given to endless practice.

> You'd go round to Barry's place and he'd have no records or
> record player, but had a room with nothing in it except for

a music stand and manuscript paper filled with bass scale exercises. He would practice them every day and this would allow him to come up with new innovative parts.[2]

Barry Sullivan was playing guitar in a band called Thursday's Children, when he swapped to bass, Tim Piper exchanging his Fender Jazz for his own Strat. According to Little Goose, Big Goose shows up at their St Kilda digs with a longer-than-usual guitar case, the square case of the Fender, on the day of the moon landing in 1969, and the two spend the next few months rehearsing, learning to play together, as a rhythm section, while Big Goose learned to master bass. Phil told me they would pick an album and learn it note for note, Booker T: Duck Dunn and Al Jackson, Cream, Hendrix, the exemplary rhythm section duos of the time or songs of the moment, like 'The Hunter'. Little Goose remembers that he and Big Goose were together in the Wild Cherries over the summer of 1968/9, BG then still on guitar. They then lived together in a house near Rippon Lea in St Kilda, nicknamed The Asylum. The band lived there, with a practice room where the Geese had meshed. Various other musos would come and join in – Mark Kennedy, Kevin Murphy, Billy Thorpe, Doug Parkinson, Billy Green.[3] The two Geese became lockstep, and able even more than might otherwise have been common to anticipate, to read each other's minds, change time or pattern intuitively or sympathetically. Big Goose had taught himself bass in union with Little Goose. They were welded together. So it was a surprise when Little Goose quit Chain, to move on to jazz, alone of the pair, but this also opened the possibility of BG's emergence as Australia's premier funk bass player, pre-eminently with soul singer Renee Geyer, first as Sanctuary and Mother Earth playing together with Mark Punch, Mal Logan and Greg Tell. For a taste, try *Really Love You*, especially, and *Ready to Deal*.[4] Later in life Big Goose was the bass player of choice for touring acts such as Little River Band and John Farnham. His musical legacy is continued by his son, Shannon, on drums and by every local bass player who ever picked up.

# *Personal

And us? I first saw Chain at Traffik, 471 Flinders Lane in Melbourne in 1970, when I was in high school, Year 11. This was the four piece with Warren, Phil and the Geese, just after *Live Chain*, 'Black and White', 'Sweet Little Angel' and 'Gertrude Street Blues'. It was the first time I saw Little Goose and those dancing hands: I knew immediately he was a jazz drummer, trained, unlike me, left hand as busy as his right, this even though he had a pin in his right after the proverbial rock band car accident. By 1971 we were in Year 12, playing support for Chain at school dances, having played earlier via Lobby with Finnen at the Thumpin Tum just into 1970. There were different line-ups and patterns of engagement. I saw Chain maybe fifty times across this period, mainly in those small clubs but also in beer barns as the shift to pub rock accelerated, as well as at various university and college gigs. We would always say hello, at least until the band really took off, and was always off to the next gig across town. The big hit, of course was that line-up, Phil, the Geese and Matt. Later, there was a three piece, piano, bass, drums cooking up a storm; Pig was now using a portable baby grand. I don't think he was much influenced by Elton John, but the arrival of Elton's power piano trio at Radio City Music Hall in *17.11.1970* on the album of that name helped open new doors, away from the guitar trio, and after all, the piano trio format was a jazz standard, as they all played jazz – so the fit was there. On one of these occasions Phil offered us a salute over their PA, as we finished our last number, giving way to them: 'It's great hearing young guys like that playing jazz! Lets hear it for them!' You could say I made this up, but both our guitarist, Scott Browne, and bass player, my brother Fred, also remember it, word for word. I thank them for the times, and for the memory check; and I send a shout-out to them and to Dave Mutton on flute. Some of this other atmospheric stuff I have checked against the diary notebooks I kept for my girlfriend and later first wife, Dor, who lived through and tolerated this youthful excess and its obsessions with grace. We would chat then in the breaks, especially to Phil. I remember saying to him after one gig that he was playing like Hendrix for the night – those ninths! Sure, he said, offering me a swig of his sauternes, I was listening to Hendrix this afternoon! So I met the idea of mimesis; as you hear, so you play, and then some. Pilgrimage, Warren and Phil, later played at lunchtime at Croydon High School, including Q and A, all this organized by local schoolboy entrepreneur Chris Pain. They were our people, we were their tribe.

Thinking back on these days, and revisiting my now slim stack of vinyl I was surprised not to find *Toward the Blues* there, alongside Beano and Blind Faith, *Wheels of Fire* and *Two of a Kind*, as well as the first album, *Chain Live*. What happened to my copy? Lost? My brother Fred remembered. We gave it to him for his twenty-first, just after it was released, October 1971, throwing a final party and playing at our folks' home before it was time to leave, too much volatility, Vietnam and all that. December 1971 I left home to live with Fred in Serene House in Lilydale, our own little Big Pink (ours was green). We shared lots, clothes, food, music, books, boots, other stuff. And we shared that album, which he still has. I found some pristine copies in vinyl shops during the writing of this book, and shared them with Phil Manning when I interviewed him at his home in West Footscray fifty years later. It's a long time back. Now we are drinking tea, and it still feels like yesterday. We listened through the tracks together, me waxing lyrical, Phil more restrained, sober, indeed. *Toward the Blues* has a long tail. We were so much older then, we're younger than that now, perhaps.

# *Tags

Period rock books include Toby Cresswell and Martin Fabinyi, *The Real Thing* (2000); Ian Marks, Iain Macintyre, *Wild about You* (2010); David Johnston, *The Music Goes Round My Head* (2010); Ian McFarlane, *The Encyclopedia of Australian Rock and Pop* (1999); David Nichols, *Dig* (2005); Iain McIntyre, *Tomorrow Is Today – Australia in the Psychedelic Era, 1966–1970* (2006); Ed Nimmervoll, *Friday on My Mind* (2004). Murray Engelheart, *Blood Sweat and Beers* (2010), is especially good on the atmospherics of pub rock. On the emergent culture of sharpies, Melbourne gangs and their music see Sian Supski and Beilharz, 'So Sharp You could Bleed – Sharpies and their Artistic Representations. A Moment in the Seventies History of Melbourne', in A. Michelsen ed., *SocioAesthetics* (2015) and 'Tricks with Mirrors: Sharpies and Their Representations', in S. Baker et al. eds, *Youth Cultures and Subcultures* (2015); Beilharz, 'Lobby and Me', *Thesis Eleven* 91, 2007, and 'Rock Lobster', *Thesis Eleven* 109, 2012; Beilharz, Supski and Greg Macainsh, 'From Sharpies to Skyhooks', *Thesis Eleven* 144, 2018.

For background, including photos and bios: back to the early 60's, see *Go!*, the label and TV show, which has a box set of CDs; and an unrelated book by Seamus O'Hanlon and

Tanya Luckins, *Go! Melbourne in the Sixties* (2005). On the longer history of vinyl, see Clinton Walker, Trevor Hogan, Peter Beilharz, 'Rock 'n' Labels. Tracking the Australian Record Industry in the Vinyl Age', *Thesis Eleven* 109 and 110, 2012. Photo books include Rennie Ellis, *No Standing Only Dancing* (2008); *Carol Jerrems – Up Close* (2010); Phillip Morris, *From AC/DC to Zappa* (2015). Biographies include Billy Thorpe, *Most People I Know* (1998); *Sex and Thugs and Rock n Roll* (1996); Lynn Thorpe and Dino Scatena, *Billy Thorpe, Keep Rockin'* (2010); Jason Walker, *Billy Thorpe's Short Time on Earth* (2009); Peter Evans, *Sunbury* (2017); Murray Walding and Nick Vukovic, *Plastered* (2007); Andrew Stafford, *Pig City* (2006); Glenn Wheatley, *Paper Paradise – Do What You Wanna Do* (2022); Renee Geyer, *Confessions of a Difficult Woman* (2000); John du Bois, *The Dingoes Lament* (2012); Broderick Smith, *Man Out of Time* (2018). The best work on Lobby Loyde is by Paul Oldham, as in 'Lobby Loyde – Godfather of Oz Rock', *Thesis Eleven* 109, 2012. See also Shane Homan, *The Mayor's a Square*, on Sydney (2003); and for some British parallels, Andy Bennett, *British Progressive Pop, 1970–1980* (2020).

Work on Australian history of the period is relatively scattered, which is surprising given the formative nature of the period. See Frank Moorhouse, *Days of Wine and Rage* (1980), Donald Horne, *Time of Hope* (1980); Frank Crowley, *Tough Times – Australia in the Seventies* (1986) Michelle Arrow, *Friday on Our Minds* (2009); Alison Pressley, *Living in the Seventies* (2002); Jennifer Clark, *Aborigines and Activism* (2008); Robin Gerster and Jan Bassett, *Seizures of Youth* (1991); Shirleene Robinson and Julie Ustinoff, eds, *The 1960s in Australia* (2012). Capsules are in Beilharz on the 60's and 70's and Walker on rock and roll music in Beilharz and Trevor Hogan, eds, *Sociology – Antipodean Perspectives* (2012).

Primary documents of social history from the period include Robert Hughes, *Art in Australia* (1970); Donald Horne, *The Lucky Country* (1964); Geoffrey Blainey, *The Tyranny of Distance* (1966); Robin Boyd, *The Australian Ugliness* (1960); Hugh Stretton, *Capitalism, Socialism and the Environment* (1976); Germaine Greer, *The Female Eunuch* (1970); Miriam Dixson, *The Real Matilda* (1975); Anne Summers, *Damned Whores and God's Police* (1976); Humphrey Mc Queen, *A New Britannia* (1970); CD Rowley, *The Destruction of Aboriginal Society* (1970); Kevin Gilbert, *Because a White Man Will Never Do It* (1973); and the ABC Boyer Lectures for 1968 (W.H. Stanner), and 1980 (Bernard Smith).

Key music narratives include the project of Clinton Walker, *Suburban Songbook* (2021*), Buried Country* (2000), *Golden Miles* (2005), *Stranded* (1996), *Inner City Sound* (1982), *History Is Made at Night* (2012). Stuart Coupe offers a trilogy: *Promoters* (2003), *Roadies* (2018), *Gudinski* (2015). Christine Bailey, *Blues Portrait: A Profile of the Australian Blues Scene*, three volumes – is a labour of love (2019, 2021); Jon Stratton, *Australian Rock* (2007), *Anthology of Australian Albums* (2020), *Hunters and Collectors – Human Frailty* (2022); Craig Horne, *I'll Be Gone* (2020), *Roots* (2019).

Gil Matthews's Aztec Music Project reissues provides wonderful remasters and memoirs, including detailed cover notes, as in Lobby, Thorpie, Carson, Chain and other discs such as *Three Aztecs and a Chain* (2015) and *Puffing Billy and Thumpin Pig Downunda*, orig. 1973, including Phil and Big Goose. Period press includes *Go Set*; *Daily Planet*, *Revolution* and *Nation Review*. A useful survey is *Long Way to the Top*, ABC TV series 2001, six episodes; and see James Cockington's books, *Long Way to the Top* (2001); and *Mondo Weirdo – Australia in the Sixties* (1992*) Mondo Bizarro – Australia in the Seventies* (1994).

There is some fine footage available of Chain via *YouTube*. The best period material is on *GTK*, c.1971, and see the Mushroom Evolution Concert 1982: Gudinski introduces. Chain are having fun playing really well with a massive audience, 10,000 or so at Myer Music Bowl in Melbourne. Songlist: *Toward the Blues* and 'I Remember' a decade on. *Laneway* 2020 features Chain's fiftieth anniversary, Musicland 2018. Studio 22, *Laneway* 2016, features the *Toward the Blues* line-up with du Bois having replaced Big Goose, Little Goose athletic and playing Drouyns, the Brisbane-made drums he played as a boy. This segment includes new music and interviews. Matt Taylor is interviewed on Gary Dunn, *The Profile* 2018, Episode 44 for WA content. See also Episode 15, Dave Hole, and Episode 20, Lindsay Wells. Matt's webpage is Matt Taylor – 'Home of Oz Blues'. Phil's is the Phil Manning Homepage. Phil is interviewed on *Laneway* 2017. There is a Chain interview on *Australian Musician* 2019, and another on *Wrokdown* 2021, as well as the *Long Play* series, Oz Music Vault 2022. See also Gil Matthews on *Wrokdown*. Harry Brus has been archiving rare materials on the net for years. Christine Mintrom exhibits interview materials on *Kiwi Musicians in Australia*. The oldest established resource is *Milesago*.

# *Thanks

I interviewed Phil Manning over February and March 2020, and exchanged endless emails and coffee with him over the next two years – thanks, Phil! Phil was the primary informant for this study, and I am grateful to him. Matt Taylor read the manuscript later, and added his blessing. Glyn Davis gave me time and insight to listen through the tracks together and help teach me about music as it is played. Jon Stratton invited me to join the 33.3 Oceania list. The Bloomsbury staff in New York–Leah Babb-Rosenfeld and Rachel Moore – were amazing, kind and patient. Thanks to Shamli Priya and the Integra production team of Pondicherry. My earlier Vinyl Age co-conspirators, Clinton Walker and Trevor Hogan, danced with me lockstep. Sian Supski lived through the resurrection of this moment; Dor Beilharz through the original experience. I am grateful to them both, as to our children, Nikolai, Rhea and Savannah, and our youngest small drummers, Teddy and Margie. I thank my band mates from 1971: Fred Beilharz, Scott Browne and Dave Mutton; and in 2022 Glyn, Nick Reynolds and Rod Neilsen. Finally, the lyrics of 'Black and Blue' and 'I Remember When I Was Young' are quoted by kind permission of Matt Taylor and Phil Manning.

Readers: special thanks to Phil Manning; Matt Taylor; Glyn Davis; Trevor Hogan; Clinton Walker; Jon Stratton; Chris Robbins; Fred Beilharz; Scott Browne; Frank Bongiorno; Sean Scalmer; Patrick McMillin; Eduardo de la Fuente; Lars Pettersson; John Rundell; Rhea and Nikolai Beilharz; at beginning, and end, Sian Supski.

# Notes

## Preface

**1**    Bob Stanley, *Yeah Yeah Yeah: The Story of Modern Pop* (London: Faber, 2013).

## Chapter 1

**1**    Michael Gudinski, 'Foreword', in *I Remember When I Was Young*, ed. Matt Taylor, Phil Riseborough, Toby Burrows (Sydney: High Voltage, 2021), np.

**2**    Barry Harvey, *The Text of Music Phrase: Fully Written Drum Set Charts, Sight Reading and Phrasing for All Instruments* (Fairfield, Queensland: self-published, 1994).

**3**    John Hepworth, *1971-Never A Dull Moment* (New York: Bantam, 2017); Loren Glass, *Carole King: Tapestry* (New York: Bloomsbury, 2021).

## Chapter 2

**1**    Santi Elijah Holley, *Nick Cave: Murder Ballads* (New York: Bloomsbury, 2021).

**2**    Andrew Stafford, *Pig City: From the Saints to Savage Garden* (St Lucia: University of Queensland Press, 2006).

**3** Greg Lawrie, in conversation with Ian Mc Farlane, cover notes to Aztec CD reissue, *Carson on the Air*, 1973/2009, np.

**4** Taylor et al., *I Remember When I Was Young*, np.

**5** Brittany Jenke, 'Chain – Toward the Blues', *Rolling Stone Australia: Top 200 Albums* (2022): 186.

**6** Ibid.

**7** O'Donnell, Toby Creswell, Craig Mathieson, John O Donnell, *Best 100 Australian Albums* (Melbourne: Hardie Grant, 2010): 182.

**8** Harvey, *The Text of Music Phrase*, 48.

**9** Clinton Walker, *Suburban Songbook: Writing Hits in Post-war/Pre-Countdown Australia* (Sydney: Golden Tone, 2021).

**10** Peter Evans, *Sunbury. Australia's Greatest Rock Festival* (Melbourne: Melbourne Books, 2017): 148.

**11** Murray Walding and Nick Vukovic, *Plastered: The Poster Art of Australian Popular Music* (Melbourne: Miegunyah Press, 2007): 88–93.

**12** Taylor et al., *I Remember When I Was Young*, np.

# Chapter 3

**1** Chris Spencer, Zbig Nowara and Paul McHenry, *Who's Who of Australian Rock!: Complete Discography of Every Group* (Noble Park: Victoria, Five Mile Press, 2002): 66.

**2** Julie Rickwood, 'Wendy Saddington and the Copperwine', in *An Anthology of Australian Albums: Critical Engagements*, ed. Jon Stratton, Jon Dale and Tony Mitchell (New York: Bloomsbury, 2020): 23–38.

**3** Karl Neuenfeldt, 'I Wouldn't Change Skins with Anybody. Dulcie Pitt/Georgia Lee, A Pioneering Indigenous Australian Jazz, Blues and Community Singer', *Journal of Jazz Research* 8, nos. 1–2 (2014): 202–22.

**4** Herbert Marcuse, *One Dimensional Man* (London: Sphere, 1964).

**5** Marybeth Hamilton, *In Search of the Blues: Black Voices, White Visions* (London: Jonathan Cape, 2007). And see David Grazian, *Blue Chicago. The Search for Authenticity in Urban Blues Clubs* (Chicago: Chicago University Press, 2003).

**6** Steve Matteo, *The Beatles: Let It Be* (New York: Bloomsbury, 2004): 40. Henry Thomas first recorded the song for a different audience and moment in 1928.

**7** Evans, *Sunbury*.

**8** David Johnston, *The Music Goes Round My Head* (Melbourne: Independent Publications, 2010): 315.

**9** Murray Engelheart, *Blood, Sweat and Beers: Oz Rock from the Aztecs to Rose Tattoo* (Melbourne: HarperCollins, 2010): 50.

**10** Ian Port, *The Birth of Loud: Leo Fender, Les Paul, and the Guitar Pioneering Rivalry That Shaped Rock 'n' Roll* (New York: Scribner, 2019): 219.

**11** Engelheart, *Blood, Sweat and Beers*, 50.

# Chapter 4

**1** George Seddon, *Landprints* (Melbourne: Cambridge University Press, 1997) 222.

**2** Michelle de Kretser, *Scary Monsters* (Sydney: Allen & Unwin, 2021).

**3**    Walker, *Suburban Songbook.*

**4**    David Johnson, *The Music Goes Round My Head – Australian Pop Music 1964–69* (Melbourne: Independent, 2010); Ian Marks and Iain McIntyre *Wild about You– The Sixties Beat Explosion in Australia and New Zealand* (Portland: Verse Chorus, 2010); Iain McIntyre, *The Encyclopedia of Australian Rock and Pop* (Sydney: Allen and Unwin, 1999); Ed Nimmervoll, *Friday on My Mind* (Rowville: Five Mile, 2004); David Nichols, *Dig: Australian Rock and Pop Music 1960–85* (Portland: Verse Chorus, 2016).

**5**    Murray Grace and John Mills, *Jive, Twist and Stomp: WA Rock and Roll Bands of the Fifties and Sixties* (Fremantle: Fremantle Press, 2010).

**6**    Jon Dix, *Stranded in Paradise: New Zealand Rock and Roll 1965 to the Modern Era* (Auckland: Penguin, 2005); Chris Bourke, *Blue Smoke. The Lost Dawn of New Zealand Popular Music 1918–1964* (Auckland: Auckland University Press, 2010); David Eggleton, *The Story of New Zealand Rock Music* (Nelson: Craig Potten, 2003).

**7**    Clinton Walker, *Suburban Songbook;* Jon Stratton, *Australian Rock: Essays on Popular Music* (Perth: API, 2007); Craig Horne, *Roots: How Melbourne Became the Live Music Capital of the World* (Melbourne: Melbourne Press, 2019); Craig Horne, *I'll Be Gone: Mike Rudd, Spectrum and How One Song Captured a Generation* (Melbourne: Melbourne Press, 2020).

**8**    Hugh Stretton, *Capitalism, Socialism, and the Environment* (Melbourne: Cambridge University Press, 1976).

**9**    Peter Beilharz, *Transforming Labor: Labour Tradition and the Labor Decade in Australia* (Melbourne: Cambridge University Press, 1994); Peter Beilharz, *Postmodern*

Socialism: Romanticism, City and State (Melbourne: Melbourne University Press, 1994).

**10** Graeme Davison, *The Rise and Fall of Marvellous Melbourne* (Melbourne: Melbourne University Press, 1978).

**11** Craig Horne, *Roots*, 11.

**12** Pauline Bailey, 'Chris Finnen' in *Blues Portrait: A Profile of the Australian Blues Scene*, Vol. 2 (Melbourne: self-published, 2021): 79–89.

**13** Port, *The Birth of Loud*.

**14** Broderick Smith, *Man Out of Time* (Australia: Starman Books, 2018): 96, 98, 289.

**15** Greg Macainsh, 'A Massive Backline of Strauss Amps', cover notes to Festival Records, *When Sharpies Ruled*, 2015: 9.

**16** Taylor et al., *I Remember When I Was Young*, np.

**17** Ibid., np.

# Chapter 5

**1** Samara Ross, 'Unbroken Chain still linked in', *The Senior*, 21 April 2021, 17.

**2** Smith, *Man Out of Time*, 136–7.

**3** Barry Harvey, in conversation with Ian McFarlane, *Live Chain* cover notes, 2010 Aztec reissue, np.

**4** Renee Geyer, *Confessions of a Difficult Woman* (Sydney: HarperCollins, 2000).

# Index

**A**

AC/DC 15, 31, 36, 62, 73, 82

Adelaide 52, 64, 68, 77

Alcohol, *see* Booze

Allman, Duane 2, 12, 23, 71

ALP (Australian Labor Party), *see* Whitlam

Amphlett, Chrissie 62

Armstrongs Studios 45

Asylum 91

Aztecs 5, 42, 43, 47, 59, 61

**B**

Balingup, 11

Band, The 6

Bay City Union 6, 87, 98

Beano, *Bluesbreakers* Album 76, 88, 93

Beat'n Tracks 6, 89

Beck, Jeff xi, 21, 80

Beechworth 11, 56

Berry, Chuck 15, 72–3

Bigsby, 80

Birch, Ric 73

Black Allan 51

'Black and Blue', single 27–30

Bloomfield, Mike 80

Boogie 7, 19, 25, 65

Booker T and MG's 51, 91

Booze 7, 20, 25, 31, 42, 60, 83–5

Bourke, Stephanie 62

Brisbane 1, 2, 6, 20, 32, 52, 54, 56, 68, 87, 89, 90

Brown, James 18, 71, 76

Brubeck, Dave 80, 90

Buford, George 54

Butterfield, Paul 51–2, 70, 78–9, 87, 89

**C**

Canberra 35, 68

Canned Heat xv, 7, 19, 58, 83

Capewell, Mal 10, 54

Captain Matchbox Whoopee Band 28, 59, 78

Carson 19, 41, 48, 53, 83, 96

*Chain Live Again* album 49–50

Chugg, Michael 60

Clapton, Eric 2, 16, 22, 25, 70, 76–8

Clyne, Ian 10, 54

Collins, Albert 85

Combo 12, 53–4, 71–2, 80, 84

Company Caine (Co Caine) 49, 82

Cooder, Ryland 23

*Countdown* TV Show 41, 65, 75

Cream 16, 17, 25, 77, 91

Croydon 52, 76–8, 93

Croydon Merrymakers 52

Cultural nationalism 3, 27, 32, 67

**D**

Daddy Cool 4–5, 43, 61, 89
Davis, Jesse Ed 23
Deep Purple 73, 80
De Kretser, Michelle, 64
Devonport 88
Diddley, Bo 52
Dingoes 31, 90
Domino, Fats Antoine 50
Dominoes, Derek and 20
Drouyn drums 70, 97
Dylan, Bob 16, 61, 80

**E**

Easybeats 52, 73–4, 76
Egmond guitars 79

**F**

Fender guitars 1, 19, 80–1, 88, 91
Fender Rhodes, 44
Festival label, 15
Finnen, Chris 78–9, 92
Fleetwood Mac 77, 79
Footscray 94
Ford, Doug 5, 82
Framus guitars, 78
Frankston 10, 54

**G**

Geyer, Renee 37, 48, 91, 95
Gibson guitars 7, 22, 25, 45, 47, 76, 80
Green, Peter 16, 77, 80
Gretsch drums 1, 33
Gretsch guitars 80
*GTK* TV Show 41–2, 53, 73, 79, 81–2, 97

Gudinski, Michael 4, 9, 16, 50, 53, 83, 88, 96, 97
Guy, Buddy xv, 18–19, 53

**H**

Hammond B3 Organ 12, 19, 44, 80–3
Hammond, John 16
Hammond, John Jr 16, 78
Hare Krishna 57
Healing Force 39, 41–2, 60, 66
Hendrix, Jimi 2, 19, 51, 77–8, 80, 91, 93
Hepworth, John, 11–12
Hi-hat 26
Hippies 2, 11, 18, 54–9, 68
Hofner guitars 78
Hohner Clavichord 7, 44, 47, 82
Hole, Dave 6, 97
Hooker, John Lee xv, 7, 19
Hughes, Robert 27

**I**

Infinity label 15

**J**

Jacobs, Little Walter xv, 80
Jamerson, James 8
James, Elmore xv, 7, 27, 47, 72, 77
James, Skip 16, 23
Johnson, Robert 16–18, 23, 88

**K**

King, BB 9, 47, 53
King, Carole 11

King, Freddie 9, 53
Korean War 58, 64

**L**

Lawler, Jiva 35, 42, 44
Lawrie, Sleepy 10, 23, 46
Led Zeppelin 41, 74, 77
Lee, Georgia 51–2
Lees, Vivian 7, 79
Lingiari, Vincent 27
*Live Chain* album 12, 44–5
Long Way to the Top 36, 73, 96
Loved Ones xv, 54, 82
Loyde, Lobby 5, 29, 32, 43, 46–7,
    75, 81, 83, 87–9, 92–5

**M**

MacCausland, Ian 33, 57
Mackenzie Theory 53, 90
Madison, Pee Wee 10, 51
Mahal, Taj 23, 51
Mahavishnu Orchestra 53, 72
Manfred Mann 3, 73
Marijuana 3, 10, 34, 44, 20, 21,
    34, 43, 49
Marine band harp, 33
Marshall amps 70, 77, 80, 81
Mason, Glyn 6, 43, 49
Masters Apprentices 5, 82
Maton guitars 24, 46, 70
Max Merritt, Meteors 47, 64, 66
Mayall, John xv, 70, 76, 79
Melbourne scene 1, 2, 5, 40–1,
    53, 62, 68–9, 84
Mighty Mouse 89
Mimesis 70, 90, 93
Montgomery, Wes 24

Morello, Joe 8, 90
Morgan, Warren 43, 48, 49–50
Morris, Russell 5, 48–9
Mouseketeers 26
Mushroom label 9, 16, 75, 97

**O**

Oz blues 85, 88, 97
Oz indigo 85, 88
Oz rock 61, 65, 73, 85, 95

**P**

Perth 6, 73
Political economy 67–9
Prog rock 6, 45, 65, 83
Pub rock 2, 3, 31, 61, 65, 92, 94
Punk 65, 68
Purple Hearts 52, 81, 88

**R**

Raitt, Bonnie 23
Reed, Jimmy 15, 52, 72, 78, 87
Rickenbacker guitars 80
Rippon Lea 91

**S**

Saddington, Wendy 28, 41,
    47–9, 51, 62, 75, 89
Sayers, John 15, 20
Seddon, George 63–4
Serenity 12, 92–3
Sessions 3, 15, 41, 45, 48
Sharpies 62, 68, 94
Shepp, Archie 42
Sid Rumpo 53
Skyhooks 4, 43, 61, 94
Slide guitar 8, 16, 19, 21–3, 37

Smith, Broderick 31, 52, 95
Spectrum 3–5, 43, 60, 66, 75, 82
Spencer, Jeremy 77
St Kilda 83, 91
*Straight as a Die* album 54–9
Strauss amps 1, 22, 88, 105
Suck More Piss 60–1 *see* Booze
Sunbury Festival 59–61, 65, 95
Supski, Sian 94, 98
Sydney 8, 15, 43, 45, 51–2, 68, 74, 76, 81

**T**
TCS studios 1
Tedeschi Trucks xi, 16, 20, 71
*Text of Music Phrase* 8, 90, 99
Thorpe, Billy 28, 43, 48, 60, 91, 95
Tilders Dutch 48, 79
Tully 81–2
*Two of a Kind* album 53–4

**V**
Vanda/Young 73, 82
Vase amps 1, 24, 70

Vietnam War 10, 11, 27, 32, 46, 50, 56, 64, 74–5, 93
Vox amps 19, 79, 81

**W**
Wah wah pedal 8, 19, 22, 36, 37, 49
Walker, Clinton 28, 37, 65, 66, 70, 98
Waters, Muddy xv, 4, 19, 25, 50, 53
Weir, Peter 28
Wells, Junior xv, 7, 18, 53
White blues 7, 19, 25, 52, 76, 85
Whitlam, E G 3, 10, 27, 67, 74
Wild Cherries xv, 32, 59, 87, 91
Wilson, Al 58
Wilson, Chris xv, 15
Winter, Johnny 12, 51, 79
Worsley, Tony 77, 88

**Y**
Youngs 73

**Z**
Zappa, Frank 5, 43, 70, 71, 78, 95